Words of Encouragement
for
Author and Readers

"Congratulations! I'll buy the first copy of your book. You did a very good job of sharing yourself and your devotion to the Little Flower. People enjoy reading other people's stories and it often gives them insight and help in their own lives. It should be a welcome message to singles and all people."
> — ***Most Reverend Joseph M. Sartoris (Bishop Joe)***
> *Archdiocese of Los Angeles*

"Your book will help a lot of people – young, single, and really, all ages and states. I wish I could write with the clarity and directness you do. It's such a worthy, evangelical endeavor."
> — ***Rev. Fr. Stephen Watson, O.C.D.***
> *Provincial, Discalced Carmelite Friars*
> *California-Arizona Province of St. Joseph*

"At the end of life, or at the end of any given day for that matter, how many of us truly say, '*Lord, You are my portion and cup, You have made my destiny secure . . . fair to me indeed is my inheritance*' *(Psalm 16:5-6 NAB)*? Yet Teresita addresses this desire of every heart with stunning simplicity and practical wisdom. Each of our lives can be enriched with a prayerful reading of this Littleways journey."
> — ***Sr. Regina Marie, O.C.D.***
> *Vicar General, Carmelite Sisters of the Most*
> *Sacred Heart of Los Angeles*

"God has truly been working in your life! Your life of prayer and love will help you write your book, which so many people need to read. With so many blessings, now we step out even more confidently and bravely to radiate the peace and joy of Christ."
> — ***Rev. Fr. Donald Kinney, O.C.D***.
> *Translator in English of "The Poetry of Saint*
> *Thérèse of Lisieux", ICS Publications, Washington DC*

"How nice to read from you! I see that there will be one more book to suggest to our English speaking pilgrims."
— ***Laurence Panontin***
Assistant to the Rector, Sanctuary of Lisieux

"Please be assured of our daily prayers and sacrifices for you and your special intentions. Let us know how the book is doing. We love you dearly!"
— ***Carmelite Nuns***
Carmel of St. Teresa, Alhambra, California

"St. Thérèse is an example of a way of life for all of us – simplicity and prayer. Thank you for such a strong reminder of how to live a holy and blest life!"
— ***Monsignor Lloyd Torgerson***
Pastor, St. Monica Catholic Community
Santa Monica, California

"Aunts and uncles are very important to the family institution. You got a good thing going in your book!"
— ***Rev. Fr. David Guffey, CSC***
National Director, Family Theatre Productions

"Beautiful manuscript, Terri, and wonderful story!"
— ***Ellen Gable Hrkach***
President 2012-2015, Catholic Writers Guild
Award-winning, Best-selling author

"This message is so needed, and its truth is so powerful. I'm grateful that Terri Ong has brought together Thérèse's story with our need for accompaniment."
— ***Vinita Hampton Wright***
Author, "The Art of Spiritual Writing"

"Good luck on your project. I am grateful and deeply touched that you found my material helpful to you." (See Appendix, page 113)
— ***Susan Muto, Ph.D.***
Renowned Author, Speaker, Teacher
2014 Awardee, Catholic Library Association

In The Footsteps of
St. Thérèse

How To Be Single But Not Alone

A Littleways Journey
Teresita "Terri" Ong

1-28-17

Rachel, may St. Therese
shower you with many roses!
Love, Terri

Unless otherwise noted, quotes from the writings of St. Thérèse are taken with permission from *Story of a Soul*, translated by John Clarke, O.C.D. Copyright (c) 1975, 1976, 1996 by Washington Province of Discalced Carmelites, ICS Publications, 2131 Lincoln Road, N.E. Washington, DC 20002-1199 U.S.A. www.icspublications.org

Drawing on page 99 from
Carmelite Spiritual Center, Darien, Illinois
Used with permission.

"Shower of Roses" drawings by the
Discalced Carmelite Nuns
Lafayette, Louisiana
Used with permission.

Cover photo of St. Thérèse
Date: April 1888
Copyright © Central Office of Lisieux
Used with permission.

Cover design by Sigmund Torre

Edited by:
Nina R. Messina
Ellen Gable Hrkach

Published by Littleways
www.littleways.com
Marina del Rey, California
Printed in the United States of America

Dedication

In loving memory of my Mommy. Thank you for teaching me how to accept my "roses."

In loving memory of Papa; my aunt Tia Ayong; my brother-in-law Bert; and all my deceased relatives and friends.

To my 2 brothers, Butch and Eddie; my 3 sisters, Ching, Odette, and Sony; my sisters-in-law, Mila and Joji; and my brother-in-law, Badong.

To my next generation nephews and nieces – all 18 of you! Being single and bearing no children, you were the first ones to whom I thought of leaving this legacy. But our family has now gone on to a third and fourth generation, and I can no longer count "us" on my fingers and toes! We are now also spread all over the globe. So to all my family anywhere and everywhere, I dedicate this book. May the faith of Felicidad A. Ong (my Mommy, your grandma, your great-grandma) live on! Let us always remember that her name, "Felicidad," which means "happiness," is what she always wanted us to have and to give to this world.

Finally, I dedicate this book to all those who ARE single and feel alone, and all those who ARE NOT single but feel alone.

Author's Note to Readers

Thank you for your interest in this book. It is not my life story I wish for you to dwell on. If I can inspire you to read (or re-read) St. Thérèse's "Story of a Soul," and even more, encourage you to trace your life story alongside hers, it will be the best "review" for this book. May God bless you! I pray that you will receive a shower of roses from the Little Flower in heaven.

Contents

Preface

Who is St. Thérèse

St. Thérèse (also known as "The Little Flower") was born in Alençon, France in 1873. She entered the Carmelite convent in Lisieux at a tender age of 15, and lived a hidden life of prayer. She grew in great intimacy with God, and remained faithful to Him throughout her earthly life. She was rooted in our Heavenly Father's powerful love, and her life was marked with unshakeable confidence and abandonment to the will of the Divine Master. She believed that what mattered in life are not great deeds, but great love. She died in 1897 at the age of 24.

The world came to know St. Thérèse through her autobiography "Story of A Soul" where she described her life as "a little way of spiritual childhood." It is easy to conclude that in the short period of her life, she could not have accomplished much. But in 1925 (28 years after her death), she was canonized a Saint of the Church by Pope Pius XI, and in 1997 (100 years after her death), she was declared a Doctor of the Church by St. Pope John Paul II. What does it mean to be a Doctor of the Catholic Church? It means that her teachings are very sound, worthy and recommended to be followed.

In sharing her life story, St. Thérèse allowed me to remember my own story alongside hers. In doing so, she pointed out Jesus to me, and helped me to see that our Heavenly Father was always with me. Although I have remained single throughout my life, God in His goodness, has never left me alone even in a blink of an eye, from the day I was born up to the present, and where I will go hereafter. The Little Flower also taught me the "language of prayer" whereby I can now say that I am – "always a bridesmaid, never a bride, living happily ever after!"

What This Book Is About

In this book, I present the "little way" of St. Thérèse as a means by which one can find happiness in the single state of life. As I grew in years and walked the "solo" road, I got to know my patron saint, St. Thérèse of Lisieux, and I found "being single" ultimately fulfilling. However, this happened only when, by following in the footsteps of St. Thérèse, I was able to accept Jesus, and He became my life partner. St. Thérèse has given us a means to grow in love with Jesus who presents Himself to us as the Bridegroom. When I take His hand as I walk my path, I recognize that even I can make a difference in this world. Oh yes, one can be "single but not alone."

There are many well-written books available about St. Thérèse which analyze her autobiography, "Story of A Soul." My book is not intended to re-phrase or summarize her book. I may do injustice to her teachings if I do that. I highly recommend to the readers of this book that they read her life story and learn directly from her. My story is simply a testimony of what she has done in my life. Herein, I humbly offer and sprinkle throughout reflections on the "journey of my soul" as I found my vocation as a single woman by following in the footsteps of St. Thérèse. I do not wish to draw attention to myself, but merely to illustrate how one can find, and continue to find, happiness in what I call *"A Littleways Journey"* (my journey).

This book is a living witness that, for a "baby boomer" like me, the "little way" of St. Thérèse still applies in the 21st century. The experiences which I share are written with a prayer that God will purify my intention to be like that of my role model, St. Thérèse, in her objective in writing her life story, although my own story is but a shadow of her "Story of A Soul."

Throughout this book, I gather quotations of St. Thérèse from John Clarke, O.C.D.'s translation of her autobiography. Every referral I make to this translation is marked "SS" with the page number(s) indicated as "p". The following is what she wrote describing the subject of her book, which is also my aim to be what this book is about.

> *"It is not, then, my life properly so called that I am going to write; it is my thoughts on the graces God deigned to grant me."* (SS, p. 15)

Who This Book Is For

When I explored the literary market due to my own need, I had difficulty finding any books or programs in the Catholic tradition focusing on the spiritual needs of singles who have never married. Although this book is primarily intended for singles who have never married, it will also be helpful to those who are in the process of discerning their vocation, and are hearing a call to the single state of life. This book will be a resource for those who wish to remain single, who live in the high tech world of "bulls" and "bears" and—let's face it—are afraid to be alone, even if one has answered the call.

Since feeling lonely is the reality of the human condition, this book will also attract those who are not single but still feel alone. During my career which spanned over three decades in the travel industry (as an airline employee; as a travel office manager; as a travel director for top Fortune 500 executives; and as a tour organizer/tour director leading Catholic pilgrimages, meetings, conventions, and international celebrations), I realized that the "little way" can speak well not only to those who are single, but to others as well. Thus, this book will be helpful to those who are in any state of life.

I have met many who were married, divorced, separated, widowed, and even priests and nuns, who were excited and expressed interest in reading about this topic when I discussed it with them. At one time in my local community, I organized a number of socials which included dining, dancing, walking, hiking, biking, and other activities. I specified that it was not a dating club, but was meant primarily to establish fellowship for singles. I was surprised to receive calls from those who were not single, but who asked if I would consider letting them join my group because they also needed support.

Besides traveling for pleasure and work, I have also lived in four countries (Philippines, Japan, Canada, and United States). As a student, it was an adventure. But when I finally emigrated from a third world country and settled in North America, I experienced enormous challenges like everyone else who assimilates into a new culture. Thus, immigrants who feel alone, having journeyed away from the land of their birth to a new place, may also be able to relate to my thoughts, prayers, and reflections that I learned from my patron saint.

This book is not limited to any age or generation; it is for all generations. However, I recognize that those who have already reached their later years may better understand what it means to be "single but not alone." As the saying goes, "with age comes wisdom."

What Need Does This Book Address

Let's be honest! Haven't we all felt alone (or lonely) at one time or another? This is the reality of the human condition. This book addresses that need. However, the need of those who have never married, (and have borne no children) is the one I address first and foremost, because this is the only state of life that I have experienced.

I once asked my dear friend, Most Reverend Joseph M. Sartoris (Bishop Joe), why the Church has nothing much in the way of programs or ceremonies to support singles. Couples have the Sacrament of Matrimony. Priests have the Sacrament of Holy Orders. Religious have ceremonies for their temporary and perpetual vows, not to mention there are many church-sponsored programs available for couples, married, separated, and divorced. A year has even been declared by the Vatican to the consecrated life. What about singles? There is nothing I have ever attended for one who has dedicated one's life to be single. Of course, those of us who are single can ask a priest to bless us when we make a commitment to live in grace. But have we ever seen a church ceremony for one who has decided to walk the aisle alone?

Bishop Joe's reply to me was something I will remember for the rest of my life. He said that there is really no need to have anything else because I have already received the Sacrament of Baptism. As a baptized person, I am enjoined in the earthly ministry of our Lord Jesus Christ.

What Led Me To Write This Book

St. Thérèse wrote her book because she was asked to do so by the Prioress at the Carmel Convent of Lisieux. The superior at that time was actually her beloved older sister Pauline, to whom

4

she wrote in confidence. Quite hesitant at first, she wrote out of obedience to her:

> *"The day you asked me to do this, it seemed to me it would distract my heart by too much concentration on myself, but since then, Jesus has made me feel that in obeying simply, I would be pleasing Him; besides, I'm going to be doing only one thing: I shall begin to sing what I must sing eternally: 'The Mercies of the Lord.'"* (SS, p. 13)

What led me to write this book? On my birthday, September 30, 2009, I remember waking up, talking to God and asking Him this question: *"Okay, Heavenly Father, we are in a recession, and I do not see much work on the horizon! Do you still have any purpose for my life?"* (I have written more about this in Chapter Five.)

Then, on April 7, 2013, I listened to a homily by Filipino Cardinal Luis Antonio G. Tagle.[1] It was the Second Sunday after Easter which was also Divine Mercy Sunday. The First Reading was from the Acts of the Apostles 5:12-16. It was about the: *"Many signs and wonders that were done among the people at the hands of the apostles."* The Second Reading was from Revelation 1:9-11a, 12-13, 17-19 about St. John on the island of Patmos and his vision of the Risen Lord, in which the author was instructed to: *"Write down, therefore, what you have seen, and what is happening, and what will happen afterwards."* The Gospel that Sunday was from John 20:19-31 about Thomas, the doubting apostle, where at the end of the Reading we are told that Jesus performed many other signs, too many for all to be written down and why: *"But these are written that you may come to believe that Jesus is the Christ, the Son of God, and that through this belief you may have life in his name."* Cardinal Tagle tied together all the Readings in a way that made me want to write even more about the journey of my soul. He said:

> *"The Risen Lord tells us, you have experienced the signs and wonders of my presence in your life, write it down, narrate it, proclaim it to the world so that others may believe in the Resurrection through you. Do it*

*please, tell the stories of your wonderful encounters
with the Risen Lord."*

And so, following in the footsteps of St. Thérèse, what has led me
to write this book is "obedience"—obedience after I listened to these
readings and homily—the Word and the Gospel of the Lord. My hope
is that, as I do so, the readers of this book will also remember their
own stories and "write it!"

Why I Am Writing This Book

If in this book I write about myself, I ask the readers to forgive
me. It is only because I am still learning how to walk humbly in my
patroness' footsteps. My prayer is that someday I will be able to say
purely, like she did, why she wrote her book:

> *"It seems to me that if a little flower could speak,
> it would tell simply what God has done for it without
> trying to hide its blessings. It would not say, under the
> pretext of a false humility, it is not beautiful or without
> perfume, that the sun has taken away its splendor and
> the storm has broken its stem when it knows that all
> this is untrue. The flower about to tell her story
> rejoices at having to publish the totally gratuitous gifts
> of Jesus. She knows that nothing in herself was
> capable of attracting the divine glances, and His mercy
> alone brought about everything that is good in her."*
> (SS, p. 15)

> *"O Mother, how different are the ways through
> which the Lord leads souls! In the life of the saints, we
> find many of them who didn't want to leave anything
> of themselves behind after their death, not the smallest
> souvenir, not the least bit of writing. On the contrary,
> there are others, like our holy Mother St. Teresa, who
> have enriched the Church with their lofty revelations,
> having no fears of revealing the secrets of the King in
> order that they may make Him more loved and known*

by souls. Which of these two types of saints is more pleasing to God? It seems to me, Mother, they are equally pleasing to Him, since all of them followed the inspiration of the Holy Spirit, and since the Lord has said: 'Tell the just man ALL is well.' Yes, all is well when one seeks only the will of Jesus, and it is because of this that I, a poor little flower, obey Jesus when trying to please my beloved Mother." (SS, p. 207)

Like my patron saint, the writing of this book is an endeavor that I undertook for the greater honor and glory of God. It is my way of giving back to the world the many blessings and joys of my life. I hope that I can pass on to my readers, especially to the "single but not alone," that even in this day and age, we can be happy. Furthermore, we do not need to accomplish big things. Even in our own "littleways," following in the footsteps of St. Thérèse, we can make a difference!

A Word About "Littleways"

Littleways is a fully registered and certified professional name under which I operate. As my work progressed, and I was asked by the Carmelite Order to organize special pilgrimages and international celebrations honoring Carmelite saints, I found my calling to be that of promoting the "little way" of St. Thérèse. In order to be creative, I joined the 2 words "little ways" into the name I use for all my work: "Littleways." To every travel program I put together and regardless of the destination, I added this tagline: "A Littleways Journey." I usually sign off my work with this quote from St. Thérèse: "It is the little things we do out of love that charm the heart of the good God." Now as an author, I also find it most appropriate to add "A Littleways Journey" to the title of this book. "A Littleways Journey" simply refers to my humble attempts to follow in the footsteps of my patron saint, St. Thérèse!

How I Am Writing This Book

Each chapter addresses specific periods in the life of St. Thérèse and how I recall similar periods of my life when her example helped me, or when I could have done better had I followed in her footsteps. So, I introduce each chapter with two small sections:

"In the Footsteps of St. Thérèse"
(St. Thérèse's Journey)

This contains a quotation(s) from the life of St. Thérèse about her "little way" - a way of spiritual childhood and complete trust. I start each chapter by letting her talk to us in her own words.

"A Littleways Journey"
(Author's Journey)

This is a summary of periods in my life contained in the chapter. Recalling and narrating my stories are intended merely to illustrate how the teachings of St. Thérèse helped me in my own *Littleways* journey of learning "how to be single but not alone!"

Then, at the end of each chapter, I have two small sections:

"Dear St. Thérèse,"
(Author to St. Thérèse)

This is a short note or prayer to tell her how I did in following (or not following!) in her footsteps in that chapter.

"Write It Down!"
(Reader's Journey)

This contains a few questions for the readers in order to trigger memories of their own life experiences. Every person who walks this earth has a precious story to tell. I encourage the readers to remember their very own stories like I did, because doing so brings to light God's loving presence in our lives. By sharing our stories, we become testimonies and transmitters of God's love to the next generation(s).[2]

Chapter One: Introduction

"In the Footsteps of St. Thérèse"
(St. Thérèse's Journey)

"It was He who had her born in a holy soil, impregnated with a virginal perfume. It was He, too, who had her preceded by eight Lilies of dazzling whiteness. In His love He wished to preserve His little flower from the world's empoisoned breath." (SS, p. 15-16)

"God was pleased all through my life to surround me with love, and the first memories I have are stamped with smiles and the most tender caresses. But although He placed so much love near me, He also sent much love into my little heart, making it warm and affectionate." (SS, p. 17)

"I was very proud of my two older sisters, but the one who was my ideal from childhood was Pauline. . . . I had often heard it said that surely Pauline would become a religious, and without knowing too much about what it meant I thought: 'I too will be a religious.' This is one of my first memories and I haven't changed my resolution since then!" (SS, p. 20)

"A Littleways Journey"
(Author's Journey)

In this chapter, I recall with my patron saint my family background and the period from my birth to my teen years. But oh, how I dreaded becoming an "old maid!"

The Heavenly Garden

How can a young adult, who did not even live a full quarter of a century, be a role model for me, a mature adult, who has reached and has lived more than double her lifetime? It would be easy to say, "She was just a kid! How could she know better?" In 1914, about 17 years after her death, Pope Pius X signed the Decree for the Introduction of the Cause of St. Thérèse's sainthood, endorsed her writings, and called her "the greatest saint of modern times." I am writing this book in 2015. It would cause one to wonder if this description of St. Thérèse, made 101 years ago, could still be true today. Well . . . let's see! This is my favorite quote from St. Thérèse:

> *"Jesus deigned to teach me this mystery. He set before me the book of nature; I understood how all the flowers He has created are beautiful, how the splendor of the rose and the whiteness of the Lily do not take away the perfume of the little violet or the delightful simplicity of the daisy. I understood that if all flowers wanted to be roses, nature would lose her springtime beauty, and the fields would no longer be decked out with little wild flowers.*
> *And so it is in the world of souls, Jesus' garden. He willed to create great souls comparable to Lilies and roses, but He has created smaller ones and these must be content to be daisies or violets destined to give joy to God's glances when He looks down at His feet. Perfection consists in doing His will, in being what He wills us to be."* (SS, p. 14)

St. Thérèse was born in Alençon, France, on January 2, 1873 to Louis and Zélie Martin. On September 30, 1897, in the region of Normandy in France, at the Carmel in Lisieux, my patron saint passed away at a tender age of 24 years and nine months. It was on the same date, September 30, 51 years later, that I was born in Quezon City, Philippines. It has been recorded that while in the infirmary, about four months before St. Thérèse died, she had written in a letter to her dear friend Father Bellière these lines: *"I am not dying; I am entering into life!"* (SS, p. 271). I sometimes wonder if she had a part in my creation.

The holy union of Louis and Zélie Martin produced nine children, but four died in their infancy. All five remaining girls entered the religious life, including the one who later became St. Thérèse. Her parents are role model parents for all generations, and the first couple to be canonized together as saints. The celebration took place on October 18, 2015, presided upon by Pope Francis, who has placed family matters at the center of his pontificate.

I was the third child of William and Felicidad, a couple whose union was not always easy, but it was still designed in heaven. There were six of us children (two boys and four girls). Memories of our childhood are very pleasant. My family had some challenges and sometimes there were worries that there may not be enough food on the table. But God always provided for us, and very well at that. By God's Divine Providence, we were well-sheltered and we enjoyed a privileged-life compared to many others in the Philippines.

My mother was greatly devoted to St. Thérèse. She had ordered a custom-made statue of this beautiful saint, where at the bottom of the image, I found a date imprinted, "September 30, 1954" (my sixth birthday). In her room, Mommy had a special alcove and a case that protected this statue. Growing up, I remember seeing little notes or letters she left inside the case. I never read what she wrote. However, I must have inherited this same "ritual" from her. I now have the statue, which my family entrusted to me after our Mommy died in 1987. I have placed it in a very special corner in the hallway by my bedroom. Every time I have a problem or I cannot make a decision about something, I leave a note or something related to whatever I am undergoing, and place it by her statue. I smile at her image, and tell her, *"Okay, my dear sister in heaven, you take care of it!"* Well, everything I have left by her statue seems to have been taken care of, or in the course of time, has gotten resolved. And everything, no matter what it is, always turns out for my benefit. I think I know why. In front of her statue, I have a Bible, opened to the page where I have highlighted Jeremiah 29:11 - *"For surely I know the plans I have for you, says the LORD, plans for your welfare and not for harm, to give you a future with hope."* This is how I experience the devotion to St.

Thérèse that I learned from my Mommy: this saint does not let me end with her statue; she leads me directly to the Holy Scriptures.

One thing about me is that I am a big planner (although I know sometimes this can drive people crazy!). This is a gift God gave me that has helped me to become a successful tour planner and group organizer (I have written more about this in Chapter Two and Chapter Three). But what could be a virtue can sometimes also be a stumbling block. My favorite quotation from St. Thérèse has been my "radar" when it is time for me to surrender myself to God's plans. It is not always easy. But when I think of a daisy that wants to be a rose, it makes sense to me to—Let it go! I cannot be what God has not planned me to be. Oh how I wanted to find my Prince Charming and live happily ever after. But this was not what God had in mind for me.

Like St. Thérèse, my family and I lived in a wonderful neighborhood. My brothers, sisters, and I were very close. My family background was also very much like that of St. Thérèse regarding her close relationship with her siblings. We were only content when we were together. Like St. Thérèse and her siblings during their childhood, my brothers, sisters, and I also enjoyed our cousins and neighbors with whom we played and went to school. But as we all grew up, each one found his or her meaning in life. Mommy and Papa have passed away now. To this date, all six of us siblings are still alive (praise God!). Currently, two are in the Philippines, two are in the United States, and two are in Canada. All my brothers and sisters have expanded their families into the second or third generations. I am the only one who has remained single. Now I have to confess, there were many times when I wondered, "What about me?" And then I would sit back and reflect on the garden of Jesus and the flower I was made to be.

The Name

St. Thérèse's baptismal name was Marie-Françoise-Thérèse Martin. The names of her sisters who she treasured growing up with were: Marie, Pauline, Léonie, and Céline. She described each of them so lovingly in her autobiography (SS, p. 20 – 21). When St. Thérèse became a religious, she took on the name Thérèse of the Child

Jesus of the Holy Face. Her devotees have called her The Little Flower, a name that best describes her teachings.

Mommy was a very devout Catholic and on this aspect Papa always went along. Papa himself had a devotion to the Sacred Heart of Jesus. All their children had a baptismal name taken after a saint or a Catholic devotion: Rafael, Concepcion, Teresita, Lourdes, Corazon, and Eduardo. I was the one named "Teresita," after St. Thérèse.

Now everything about me was also named after my patron saint. I was born at Santa Teresita Hospital. Our parish and where I was baptized was Santa Teresita Church. And I went to school at St. Theresa's College. I don't know if this was by coincidence or something made to order in heaven! Although I am sure my parents named me after St. Thérèse, The Little Flower, the places about me could have been named after the so-called "bigger one," St. Teresa of Avila. But for me, it is still the same because the 16th century Spanish saint (Teresa of Avila) was the role model for the younger saint from France of the 19th century (Thérèse). Now here I am in the 21st century. It is my hope that my life can be worthy of those who have become my role models.

By the way, my nickname is "Titay." When I came to North America, I gave myself a new nickname: "Terri." And I tell everyone to make sure to spell it with two "R"s and an "I" at the end. I do not want it spelled with a "Y' on the end as that makes it seem like a man's name. My oldest sister once said that for people to remember how to spell my name, I just need to tell them to remember "Terri, the Terrible," that's me. But I am consoled by the fact that, in comparing Thérèse with her sister Céline, their Mamma also found that the young Thérèse's "faults shine forth with great brilliance!" (SS, p. 23)

How Will The Flower Bloom

What I found so interesting in reading about St. Thérèse's family background and her childhood was how important her relatives were to her growth, just as it has been for me and my siblings. After her mother passed away (the "crucible of trial" that she refers to and which I have written about in Chapter Two), Thérèse's father, Louis Martin, decided to leave Alençon and bring his daughters to Lisieux so they could be in closer contact with his wife's family. In Lisieux, the Martin family lived in a beautiful home named *Les Buissonnets* (meaning "little bushes"), and this was where The Little Flower bloomed until she entered Carmel at the age of 15. This was how she described her new home, and how she regarded her close relatives:

> *"I experienced no regret whatsoever at leaving Alençon; children are fond of change, and it was with pleasure that I came to Lisieux. I recall the trip, our arrival at Aunt's home; and I can still picture Jeanne and Marie waiting for us at the door. I was very fortunate in having such nice little cousins. I loved them very much, as also Aunt and especially Uncle."*
> (SS, p. 35)

I took note especially of her regard for her aunt and uncle, and I like to bring this to the attention of singles. We should never underestimate our roles in the family institution.[3] As aunts and uncles to our nieces and nephews, we also play an important part in their development, as was the case with St. Thérèse, as well as it was with me. Finally, so are cousins, as St. John the Baptist was to our Lord Jesus Christ.

Growing up, my family lived in a compound made up of three houses. The first was my mother's oldest sister's house where she lived with my two older cousins. The second was my mother's three other sisters' house, one of them widowed and the other two single, plus a dear cousin closer to our age. The third was that of my immediate family. My mother was the youngest, and her sisters all looked after her very diligently, as well as us, her six children. We all loved to hang out in the second house because there we had our very dear single aunt, Tia Ayong. (My other single aunt died when I was very young.) Tia Ayong never married and was someone we all considered our second mother. She was always home and her only daily concern was that we, all the children in the family compound, had everything we needed before we went off to school. Even cousins who lived outside the compound visited her regularly. But as much as I loved her and admired her gentle and prayerful demeanor, I always thought that I did not want to be single like her for the rest of my life!

As a young girl, I was very fat. But even though I got teased at school, I was a happy girl. One day, my mom was called to the principal's office as they were worried about my health. Mommy assured them that I was fine. She explained to them that, as a baby and up to the age of seven, I had very bad asthma. My guess is that my parents compensated for this by making sure I was well-fed. But as I reached my teens, I became more conscious of my appearance because, like the other girls, I started to have crushes on boys. My mother took me to a doctor and I was started on a diet program. Mommy also took me to swimming lessons every summer. Gradually the "fat girl" slimmed away, and then it was the boys who had a crush on me! I have to admit that there were times I wondered if St. Thérèse also had crushes on boys. I am sure boys would have had crushes on her because she was very pretty. But what she wrote, which I quote below, explains how much in love she was with Jesus even at an early age. Indeed, this makes her very relevant to all generations, because all human attraction that becomes "LOVE" is one that flows from and returns to the Sacred Heart of Jesus.

> *"I was six or seven years old when Papa brought us to Trouville. Never will I forget the impression the sea made upon me; I couldn't take my eyes off it since its majesty, the roaring of its waves, everything spoke to my soul of God's grandeur and power. I recall during the walk on the seashore a man and a woman were looking at me as I ran ahead of Papa. They came and asked him if I were his little daughter and said I was a very pretty little girl. Papa said 'Yes,' but I noticed the sign he made to them not to pay me any compliments. It was the first time I'd heard it said I was pretty and this pleased me as I didn't think I was. You always took great care, Mother, to allow me to come in contact with nothing that could destroy my innocence, and you saw to it, too, that I heard nothing capable of giving rise to vanity in my heart. As I listened to what you and Marie said, and as you had*

*never directed any compliments to me, I gave no great
importance to the words or admiring glances of this
woman. . ... I made the resolution never to wander far
away from the glance of Jesus in order to travel
peacefully towards the eternal shore!"* (SS, pp. 48 -
49. The "Mother" she addresses here is her older sister
Pauline, the Prioress of Carmel, who she had obeyed
in writing her life story.)

St. Thérèse went to boarding school, which I thank God I did not
have to, or I would have suffered much to be separated from my
family. Having already lost her mother at the age of four, she
experienced extreme loneliness in her childhood, during her school
years, as she described below:

*"I was eight and half when Leonie left boarding
school and I replaced her at the Abbey. I have often
heard it said that the time spent at school is the best
and happiest of one's life. It wasn't this way for me.
The five years I spent in school were the saddest in my
life, and if I hadn't had Celine with me, I couldn't have
remained there and would have become sick in a
month. The poor little flower had become accustomed
to burying her fragile roots in a chosen soil made
purposely for her. It seemed hard for her to see herself
among flowers of all kinds with roots frequently
indelicate; and she had to find in this common soil the
food necessary for her sustenance!"* (SS, p. 53)

The girls in my family all went to St. Theresa's College, in
Quezon City, which was just across the street from our house. It was
run by the Missionary Sisters of the Immaculate Heart of Mary who
originated in Belgium. It was a private all-girls' Catholic school. The
boys in my family went to the private all-boys' Catholic school,
Ateneo de Manila, run by the Jesuits. Both are known to have very
high educational standards. And oh yes! The nuns at my school were
strict. My guess was that they all prayed and wanted the girls to be
nuns, and the boys to be priests.

I used to wonder what was in those many layers of clothing they wore, and how they managed to stay neat and clean in their habits in spite of the hot weather in the Philippines. I loved to attend Mass at our school chapel, to listen to their communal prayers, and to join them in their singing. While I do not remember having a vision of myself as one like them in the future, I was always fascinated by the hymn that Sr. Robrecht, taught us: "The Lord is my Shepherd." I loved to sing it as it brought me a wonderful feeling each time I imagined a shepherd leading his flock with his crook and his staff, and then the sheep lying down in green pastures.

In grade school, I remember my favorite book was a geography book with a map of the United States. I memorized all the states and where they were located. I envisioned myself living "somewhere there" when I grew up. I was also fascinated with the world map and visualized myself traveling all over the globe. But this dream got confused every so often. In my late teens I dated quite regularly, and a few times I even had two young men after me. I also prayed novenas to St. Joseph and St. Anthony to "find me the right husband." But while I assumed I would get married someday, it didn't occupy my mind more than my interest in going to see the world. The nuns in school gave us many sessions bringing to our attention the subject of vocations and the three states of life. But I don't remember anyone, especially me, who cared much hearing about the single state of life. In fact, I dreaded becoming an "old maid!"

"Dear St. Thérèse,"
(Author to St. Thérèse)

How wonderful that so early in life, you heard God's call and followed it. Please watch over all singles who are hearing the call, but afraid to be alone. I am blessed to be named after you, but I have a long way to go to be like you. Please remind me always to be only the flower that God intended me to be.

"Write It Down!"
(Reader's Journey)

1.   *What was your family like? What was your school like?*

2.   *Who were you named after, and how has this affected you?*

3.   *Which of the three states of life (married, religious, single) attracted you the most in your childhood? As a teenager? And up until the first quarter of your life?*

Chapter Two: The Globetrotting Days

"In the Footsteps of St. Thérèse"
(St. Thérèse's Journey)

"I understood that to become a saint one had to suffer much, seek out always the most perfect thing to do, and forget self. I understood, too, there were many degrees of perfection and each soul was free to respond to the advances of Our Lord, to do little or much for Him, in a word, to choose among the sacrifices He was asking. Then, as in the days of my childhood, I cried out: 'My God, I choose all!' I don't want to be a saint by halves, I'm not afraid to suffer for You, I fear only one thing: to keep my own will; so take it, for 'I choose all' that You will!" (SS, p. 27)

"I had to pass through the crucible of trial and to suffer from my childhood in order to be offered earlier to Jesus. Just as the flowers of spring begin to grow under the snow and to expand in the first rays of the sun, so the little flower whose memories I am writing had to pass through the winter of trial." (SS, p. 30. This is in reference to the death of her mother at her tender age of 4 years.)

"A Littleways Journey"
(Author's Journey)

In this chapter, I remember the latter part of my teen years, then on to my 20's and 30's as a young adult, and my 40's as a mature adult. Several of my dreams have come true, and I found myself in a travel ministry, with a specific purpose, to promote the "little way" of St. Thérèse. However, I still continued to keep my eyes open hoping to find the "right husband." My mother's death was the saddest time of my life.

19

The Dream

St. Thérèse knew exactly what she wanted very early in life. Although she wrote "I choose all!" she always chose the only "ALL" that really matters – God's will. I wanted it "all" too, but I am not sure if all my dreams were always on the right track as hers were.

Who does not wish to travel? I am sure there are not many who do not have "travel" on their bucket list. Even St. Thérèse wanted to travel. She was a "dreamer" too. But in her "little way," she dreamt with full trust and abandonment to God's will. Even when she was already very ill (she suffered from tuberculosis), St. Thérèse still wished to travel, and she expressed this desire in Manuscript C, which she addressed to Mother Marie de Gonzague, her Prioress at the time of writing this portion of her book:

> *"Dear Mother, your own prudence was able to discover God's will and in His name you forbade your novices to think of leaving the cradle of their religious childhood; but you understood their aspirations since you had asked in your own youthful days to go to Saigon. It is thus that the desires of Mothers find an echo in the soul of their children. O dear Mother, your apostolic desire finds a faithful echo in my own soul, as you know; but let me confide why I desired and still desire, if the Blessed Virgin cures me, to leave the delightful oasis where I have lived so happily under your motherly care, and go into a foreign land."* (SS, p. 217)

When I was about to graduate from high school, I was a bit confused as to what to study in college. My first wish was to obtain a Bachelor's degree in Home Economics, because I thought that would make me a good wife and a mother. But this wish had to be dropped because by the time I reached college, my school had closed down the Home Economics program. My second wish was to obtain a Bachelor's degree in Foreign Service, which I did pursue, because I thought that would allow me to see the world. But even as I pursued it, I sometimes wondered if I should not have majored in Accounting instead. Being the second girl, I always felt secure following in my older sister's footsteps. She was two years ahead of me and she was obtaining a Bachelor of Science degree in Commerce with a major in Accounting. I had always looked up to my oldest sister and thought that whatever she did, I would just follow, and whatever happened in her life, would also happen to me. Unconsciously, I was trying to be the same beautiful flower that my older sister was. This was very typical of me for the first two decades of my life. In retrospect, sticking to my own interest in college was one of my early courageous acts toward following my own dreams and being the "flower" God intended me to be in His garden, as St. Thérèse described.

During this period of my life, there were three books that I enjoyed very much, which were part of my curriculum:

1) "Man's Search for Meaning" by Viktor Frankl
2) "The Little Prince" by Antoine de Saint-Exupéry
3) "Jonathan Livingston Seagull" by Richard Bach

I read them over and over again. I even got myself a poster to hang on my bedroom wall of a "Seagull" flying in the sky with a quotation from Richard Bach: *Hold fast to dreams for if dreams die, life is a broken-winged bird that cannot fly.*

But as I was getting close to graduating from college in 1970, student activism in the Philippines was gaining momentum and the Marcos regime was at its peak. There were many student teach-ins, rallies, and demonstrations. Although my school did not participate a great deal in these, there were several of us students who were very much interested in listening to what was going on. Even more so, the reason was because a student leader from one of the private Catholic boys' schools was very charismatic and some of us girls had a crush on him. But he did have good things to say about the future of our country. I was one of those moved by several speeches he made, and also by other student leaders. Several from my class were also starting to realize that our "convent days" were about to be over, and it was time to look into what we might do after graduation. As we explored, we recognized the ills of our society. I, for one, realized that in my country, as well as in other third-world countries, there was a big gap between the rich and the poor, with a very small middle class between the two. As I got more and more involved in this, I started having a desire not only to see the world, but to change the world. I had begun to understand what Viktor Frankl wrote in his book, "Man's Search for Meaning" about finding my "why." The "how" was the next big question.

In Search of Meaning

And so I thought there were only two ways I could help change the world: 1) to marry a man who would one day be a senator (or even be the future President of the Philippines!); or 2) to be a teacher. The first one was obviously a big dream beyond my control, so I went for the second. But Education was not the degree I had obtained. I prayed hard and asked my patron saint to guide me. To my surprise, soon after college graduation, the dean of my school offered me an opportunity to teach at my alma mater because one of the teachers had become ill. Providentially, another Catholic all-girls private school, Maryknoll College, also offered me a teaching position. I became a college teacher and taught History and International Studies. As these teaching jobs were only part-time, I had time to undertake further studies. I enrolled at the University of the Philippines to pursue a Master's degree in Asian Studies. I thought if I were to change the world, I would have to start first with the Orient.

Since the one who looks after me from above never fails, more doors allowing my multiple dreams to occur started to open up for me. While I was pursuing my graduate course at the university, I was one of five students granted a study tour of Southeast Asia. It was my first time getting on a plane and leaving the Philippines. Just as I was about to embark on the writing of my thesis, another wonderful opportunity opened for me. I was granted a full scholarship by the Ministry of Education of Japan to do my thesis research at the International Christian University in Tokyo. Oh what a dream come true! It was a generous scholarship with many opportunities to further my international exposure. I was assigned to live in the Foreign Student House in Tokyo, where for the first time in my life, I lived away from home, and with students who came from all over the globe. What better way would there be for me to see the world, but through the multi-cultural friends I made at the dorm. I could only thank The

Little Flower, my "sister" in heaven! She showed me how true was what she promised in the novena prayer Mommy taught me, and which I prayed very often then: *"I will let fall from heaven . . . a shower of roses."* I received my Master's degree from the University of the Philippines, and my thesis dedication page reads this way:

> *To those in search . . . "If someone loves a flower, of which just one single blossom grows in all the millions and millions of stars, it is enough to make him happy just to look at the stars." (Antoine de Saint-Exupéry, The Little Prince) . . . I dedicate this thesis.*

My thesis title was "A Cross-Cultural Study of the Social Expectations by Men of Women in Two Branches of An International Bank in Manila and Tokyo." It was a comparative study of the role of women in a developing country and in an already developed country. Interestingly, I found that Filipino women advanced more in education and careers than did Japanese women at the time of my study. I felt justified in pursuing my professional dreams as a woman.

But Robert Bach's "Jonathan Livingston Seagull" did not allow me to completely forget my dream of traveling. At the same time, a book I also enjoyed reading, "The Power of Positive Thinking" by Norman Vincent Peale taught me to *"prayerize, picturize, actualize."* I held on to an image of myself in a very smart travel outfit, suitcase in hand, boarding a plane, and traveling the world over! How could I do all of these? I had no doubt in my mind that *"I can do all things through him who strengthens me." (Philippians 4:13).* I did not allow myself to doubt that I could continue dreaming several dreams at the same time. I knew God was on my side, for after all, my dreams were well-aligned with the motto of St. Theresa's College where I spent 16 years from kindergarten through college. My school molded us to go out into the world and . . . *"Let your light shine!"*

During that time as a young adult in my 20's, even though I had begun to see the world, I continued to date. I had several suitors, including international ones. And I continued to pray my novenas to St. Joseph and St. Anthony. But no one seemed to be the one that would make me fall in love like crazy and settle down. I used to tease St. Anthony (the patron saint of finding things). I told him that he had helped me find all the contact lenses that I had dropped. Everything I lost, he helped me find; however, to this date, he still had not found me the "right husband!"

The Starting Line . . . The Little Way

The next period of my life, during my 30's and into my 40's as a mature adult, I had many "starts." At times I even found myself having to start all over again. But after many twists and turns, I finally realized my dream of traveling, immigrating to the United States and Canada, and finding myself in the travel industry wherein I found myself with a specific purpose, to promote the "little way" of St. Thérèse. And how did all of this unfold?

The Starting Line

My post-graduate research scholarship in Tokyo was just about to end, and again, I did not know what to do with my life. But God had a quick answer for me. I was offered a position at the Philippine Airlines Sales Office in Tokyo working in the Group Reservations Department. Without a second thought, I dropped all my plans to immediately go home to the Philippines to restart my teaching career. All I could think of was that after one year of working with Philippine Airlines in the Tokyo Sales Office, I would have travel benefits, not only for me, but for Mommy and the rest of the family. I took the job, and every night when I came home from work, I would look at the map and visualize taking Mommy to Rome, Lourdes, and Fatima. That dream did come true. After then I went home to the Philippines without any definite plan as to what to do next. But no sooner had I settled back than I was offered a job at KLM Royal Dutch Airlines as a Sales Representative in the Manila Branch Office. Now all I could think of again was travel benefits, and this time, from a bigger airline with a wider international network and worldwide destinations. I took the job, and for several years traveled every opportunity I could, and of course, still continued dating whenever there was someone interested in me.

Now it was actually during one of my vacation trips that I heard God 'faintly' calling me and forming me in what would later become my travel ministry. It was my vacation time, and I had planned to visit with some KLM friends in Caracas, Venezuela whom I had met at one of the inter-company sales training workshops in the Netherlands. But I had forgotten to get myself a visa to Venezuela which was necessary for a Philippine passport holder. Fortunately, my KLM Venezuelan friends had important connections in their government. They told me to just go on one of the next KLM flights from Manila to Rome, and in the meantime they would work on my visa in order to allow me to enter their country, as they needed a few days to get it all together. So I started my vacation by going to Europe with one of our KLM tour groups whose itinerary went first to the Holy Land and ended in Rome. I had never dreamt of going to the Holy Land before, and it was not even part of my immediate plans. But one day, while we were in Israel on this tour, walking by the Sea of Galilee with our Jewish guide reading from the Bible, I had a kind of "vision." It was of me coming back to the same place leading many people—groups and groups of pilgrims following me, and I, reading to them verses from Holy Scriptures. After a week in Jerusalem and Tiberias, we went to Rome and from there, I took one of our KLM flights to Caracas. I continued the next week of my vacation time and enjoyed a fantastic holiday with my South American friends in Venezuela. Indeed, I was globe-trotting! What a nice holiday I had, nothing of which I thought would have any connection to God's plan for me, not until several years afterward.

All this occurred during the late 1970's to the early 1980's when I was living and based in the Philippines. The political and economic situation in my country was getting more and more disturbing with martial law continuing and being enforced by President Ferdinand Marcos. Many Filipinos just wanted to leave the country and find greener and freer pastures elsewhere. I was like everyone else wanting to immigrate to the United States, which had been one of my childhood dreams anyway. Like the "Seagull," I held fast to that dream, and it happened.

An opportunity came up that allowed me to come to the United States on a work visa. One of the ways in which to come and live in the United States legally was to set up one's own business and work solely for that specific corporation, as this did not take any jobs away from American citizens. Of course, it cost money and required legal consultation and representation. My Mommy supported me on this venture, most of all with prayers and encouragement. Mommy was always a big supporter of the Carmelite Order. She had the whole community of cloistered Carmelite nuns in Quezon City, Philippines pray for me every day as I embarked on my new adventure.

In God's Plan

What happened next and where I found myself living seemed like a "coincidence." It was not planned that way but I ended up coming to Southern California to live, first near my American friend I had met in the dorm in Tokyo. I lived in Monterey Park close to where she lived and where we also had some other friends from our Tokyo days. As time went on and as I explored the nearby area, I found a wonderful church in Alhambra, St. Therese Church, run by the Discalced Carmelite Friars, where I enjoyed going for my daily and Sunday Masses. I had a good feeling about the parish and the neighborhood, so that as soon as my lease was up at my apartment in Monterey Park, I moved to Alhambra, very close to St. Therese Church. As I settled into my new place, it was only then I realized that on the same Alhambra Road as my parish church, and right across from my apartment complex, was the Carmel of St. Teresa of the cloistered Carmelite nuns. And just a few blocks away was the Sacred Heart Retreat House, ministered by the active Carmelite sisters. These were similar to the Carmelite nuns that my mother always supported and ran to for prayers in the Philippines. It was only much later in my life that I realized there are no coincidences. Everything happens for a purpose in God's divine plan!

The business we wanted to establish when I came to the United States, "Orient Pacific Services, Inc.," was planned originally to help nurses in the Philippines obtain work contracts from hospitals in the United States. But by God's divine intervention, one day the Provincial of the Discalced Carmelite Order who was in residence at my new parish telephoned me. Apparently they had heard of my travel background and needed help. It was early in 1982, the year of the fourth centenary of the death of St. Teresa of Avila, who was known to be a reformer of the Carmelite Order in the 16th century. The Carmelite Friars were planning a major pilgrimage to the Holy

Land and Europe, but the priest in charge was ill and needed help putting together their plans. They asked for my help—and lo and behold—later that year, in September, 1982, we took three busloads of pilgrims on an international convention and a pilgrimage program that I helped put together. It was my first real Carmelite in-depth experience and in which I also learned about Carmelite spirituality from the teachings of St. Teresa of Avila, the role model of my patron saint of the "little way," St. Thérèse of Lisieux. With that, my travel ministry began and from that time on I led many pilgrimages, mostly with the Carmelites.

My Plan

And what about my dream of getting married? Whenever I was not traveling, I spent my time looking into singles clubs in Southern California. I tried several of them. I became an officer of the Los Angeles Catholic Alumni Club, a singles club for college-educated singles wanting to meet marriageable professional Catholics. I attended numerous dances and activities, and being in charge of the club's religious activities, I once even organized a singles' weekend retreat at El Carmelo, a retreat house run by the Discalced Carmelite Friars. I also dated some eligible men from the club, until I really got tired of it. Dating and being in a relationship can be very tiring as it involves "playing a lot of games." (e.g. Is he going to call me tonight? If he does not call me, I'm not going to call him! Now whose turn is it to call? Is he going to ask me out again?)

I remember at one time, I was dating this fellow, Tim, from the club, and this other young man, Dave, from my parish. I literally dated one on a Friday, and the other on a Saturday. On Sundays, I rested. Just about that time, I was feeling pressured as my best friend, Cynthia, who I went with to all the singles dances, was finally getting married to a very nice man we met at one of the dances. We were preparing for her wedding then, and as I was her "maid of honor," she told me that I could bring a date to the wedding. My problem was— shall I ask Tim or Dave? I told myself that because this is a very special wedding, my best friend's wedding, my date would also have to be very special, the one that I would marry. So I asked God to show me which of the two it should be.

But the truth was, deep within, I really didn't think that either one of them was right for me. There were days when I thought Tim was better than Dave, and other days when I thought Dave was better than Tim. There was only one thing I was sure of: I wanted to get married, and soon! So I prayed a nine-day novena to St. Thérèse. I asked her to give me a rose during the period of my novena to serve as a sign. And I said to her that if I received a red rose, I would take it to mean that the right man for me was Dave. But if I received a white rose, which I knew was difficult to find, then it would be Tim, as it would take time before he would be ready to marry anyway.

But I did not rely on my novena alone. I tried to help St. Thérèse too, and the reason I gave myself was the cliché that "God only helps those who help themselves." I was praying the novena around Mother's Day. On Mother's Day, my friend Mary usually shared her mother with me (because my Mommy was living in the Philippines). We planned to take her mother out for brunch but since Mary was busy, she asked me to take charge of finding a good place and making the reservations. So when I heard that the Pasadena Hilton would be giving out red roses on Mother's Day, I decided that was where we should go. I thought to myself that if I smiled and was nice to the waiter, there was a good chance that I would receive a rose too. In that case, my novena would be answered with the sign that would lead me to a faster wedding. As I manipulated this, of course I did receive my so-called red rose, the sign that it would be Dave. But guess what happened! Dave couldn't make it to be my date for the wedding, as he was working that day. So I asked Tim, who was just delighted to be my date. But let me tell you a secret, neither one of them proposed.

As I look back at the crazy years of the searching stage of my life, there were two things I got for myself aimed at marriage. In 1982, when I was in Cana in the Holy Land with the three busloads on my first Carmelite pilgrimage, we had the married couples in our group renew their marriage vows. Then the Carmelite priest who was leading the trip with me, Fr. Bonaventure Galvin, O.C.D., asked the pilgrims to pause and say a very special prayer that I might find the right husband. As there were about 120 pilgrims who prayed for me, I was quite sure the Lord would hear their prayers. So I bought myself a bottle of Cana wine, which I brought home with the intention of using it at my Catholic wedding ceremony. I also bought a promising book, entitled "Your Catholic Wedding." I thought then that if I read it and envisioned images of a beautiful Catholic wedding, ("picturize" as Norman Vincent Peale said) it would happen to me. Many years passed, and as the wine was not being used, one day I decided to drink it, and sure enough, I drank it alone. And the book collected dust in my bookshelf so that after many years, I donated it to my local library.

God's Plan Wins

To make a long story short, God had a different plan for me. I tried many times to talk to Him, and to tell Him exactly what I wanted. But in a very gentle way, God was presenting a different plan for me. It was sometime in 1984 that I decided to go on a retreat at the Sacred Heart Retreat House in Alhambra. In the beautiful garden of this retreat house ministered by the Carmelite sisters, there is a statue of St. Thérèse. During that weekend retreat, I stood in front of her statue each day and had a heart-to-heart chat with her. At one time I found myself crying. I told her that I could see that the work that God was presenting to me was nice; I could travel a lot, see many exciting places, and meet many beautiful people. But it was so hard to be alone, so why could I not do it with someone—a husband? Just then, a Carmelite sister who was walking around the grounds saw me, and upon seeing tears in my eyes, approached me. I told her what I was crying about. But to my disappointment, she gave me one quick answer which made me cry even more. She said, *"Teresita, there is no right man for you in this world, because the only right man for you is Jesus."*

Oh at that moment, how I wished I could have squeezed her neck! I shall never forget her. After that, whenever I would see her, I would remind her of that conversation, but she did not remember it. Years later, however, I would look for her and then only wanted to give her a big hug because she had really helped me to find my "right man."

I went on retreat at least once a year, and each time, I felt God telling and assuring me to just trust Him. In fact, I always heard him telling me only one thing: *"See, I have inscribed you on the palms of my hands . . . "* (Isaiah 49:16). It was not easy, and there were many times when I thought God was unfair. But as the years went by, at the end of each retreat, I heard God asking me, *"Whom shall I send, and*

29

who will go for us?" and I would reply to Him, *"Here am I; send me!"* (Isaiah 6:8).

So many things happened to me in the process of trying to find happiness in being single. Many doors were closed but many doors were also opened. I tried lots of other ways to "beat" God's plans, but in the process, I only saw how God truly respects my will, and that He would never ever impose His will on me. He loves me so much that before He lets me do my will, He wants to give me a glimpse as to what He has in mind for me instead, as I might agree with Him that His plan was better.

The Little Way

During this period, I remember how I prayed for the right husband in a way that most Filipinos love to pray, that is, praying novenas to our favorite saints. Oh yes, I prayed to them all, even St. Jude, the Patron Saint of the Impossible. I also had, and still have, a little altar with statues in my bedroom, just as you will find in most Filipino homes. And if a particular saint isn't granting my requests, that statue would "respectfully" get turned around! But there was only one saint that never got turned around, the statue of St. Thérèse, The Little Flower, the one that I inherited from my Mommy. Although my patron saint did not find me the right husband, she showed me her "little way."

From my childhood, I had always had a devotion to St. Thérèse as my patron saint, but I never really knew much about her. My devotion to her up to this time which I call "The Starting Line . . . The Little Way" was a "magical" type of relationship – asking her for roses as signs when I asked God for something. I was already in my 30's when I went on that retreat, crying in front of her statue, asking for her help in meeting the right man, when I found her book, "Story of A Soul," and read it for the first time. It was then I learned about her "little way" of love and confidence in God. It is not a lonely way at all, even if one is alone. Not at all, because it is the way of spiritual childhood, of having complete trust and abandonment to the will of our Father, even to one like me who had found a dream come true, a work and, finally a ministry of traversing the world over. And so it was this "little way" that I started to take to my work, and promote to every person God sent along my way, and that I continue to promote to this day.

What is the "little way" of St. Thérèse? As I wrote in the preface of this book, there are many well-written books available about St. Thérèse which analyze her autobiography "Story of A Soul." I will not attempt to re-phrase or summarize her book, as I may only do injustice to her teachings. The best that I can do to explain her "little way" is to quote her words directly, and share my own experiences as a testimony of what she has done in my life. In doing so, it is my hope that I can also witness to the fact that she can still be relevant to a single person like me who never married, and who came to this world on the brink of the 20th/21st centuries. What makes her "little way" one to follow for all times and all generations, is simply that her way does not stop with her. Followers of her "little way" are taken straight through the heart of Jesus, to the Heavenly Father, and never left alone, and this is timeless.

Knock, Knock . . . A Rose for You

For a single person discerning one's vocation, St. Thérèse is, without doubt, a saint to be followed. Okay, I have answered God's call to dedicate my career serving Him in a travel ministry. But what about singles, who like in my situation, need to make ends meet, not only professionally, but also financially? Did St. Thérèse ever have any concerns like these? She lived "securely" in a Carmelite convent with abundant time to pray. I have to admit, these were questions I asked myself during this period of my life. Singles today in the 21st century may wonder just like I did at that time.

The late 1980's was an especially difficult time in my life. Exciting and fun though it was, my travel ministry work had numerous challenges. Financially, it was very unstable and there were times when I did not know how far I could stretch my budget. In order to establish contracts with airlines, hotels, and other partners for tour packages, I needed to make deposits well ahead of time. I had to carefully watch the capital available for the business, and rely greatly on my good credit standing and credibility within the travel industry. Oftentimes I used my personal credit cards to advance whatever was necessary. But I never knew if there would be sufficient numbers of people booking on the tours in order to break even, or if I would meet the required minimum number to proceed with a tour. I also had deadlines to consider if I were to get my deposits back. It was a considerable gamble, but I went ahead putting pilgrimage tours together especially when requested, and whenever I felt strongly that it was what God wanted me to do for Him.

In addition to financial insecurities, I was required to renew my work visa in the United States every year, and demonstrate the viability of the business. My lawyer had applied for an immigrant visa status for me, but because the waiting time for Filipino citizens was so long, it seemed as if it would never happen. Immigration, even then as it is now, is not an easy matter to endure. It can be a nightmare, almost like living in "limbo." And for one like me who is single and very far from my family, one can experience extreme loneliness, even when surrounded by good friends.

On top of this, in 1987, my beloved mother passed away. It was the saddest time of my life. I felt so lonely; all my siblings had gotten married by then, and I needed to be with family. On this matter of grief in losing Mommy, I had a companion in my patron saint, when she lost her mother at the very tender age of four. As a single person, even if I was much older than St. Thérèse when my Mommy died, I could relate very well to what she described as a "crucible of trial" about her Mamma's death. My experience was like hers which she wrote about in this way:

> *"I must admit, Mother, my happy disposition completely changed after Mamma's death. I, once so full of life, became timid and retiring, sensitive to an excessive degree. One look was enough to reduce me to tears, and the only way I was content was to be left alone completely. I could not bear the company of strangers and found my joy only within the intimacy of the family."* (SS, p. 35. The "Mother" she addressed here is her older sister Pauline, who was also her Prioress at Carmel.)

Decisions, Decisions

At that time, my youngest sister and her family immigrated to Canada. As soon as I heard this, I went to the Canadian Consulate in Los Angeles, to see if I could obtain an immigrant status to Canada. Without question, I fully qualified on my own merit, and I was granted a visa immediately. So the following year, I put all my travel ministry work in the United States on hold; I put my things in a storage location in Alhambra, and I moved to Toronto. There I immediately found a good job. I became a manager of one of the leisure travel offices of American Express. I purchased a condominium and settled in. But as always, when one thinks all is finally in order, something else comes up! To my surprise, during my third year living in Toronto, my immigrant visa petition in the United States was approved. That much prayed for "green card" was now a dream come true for me, but I had to return to the United States. What a big decision I needed to make because my life in Canada was by then well established, except that I still had not found the "right husband."

It was also around that time that I learned a valuable lesson about "happiness." Things were not going well with a fellow I was dating, and yet I wanted him to be right for me, even if I knew he wasn't. Although things were going well in my professional life in Canada, I had become worried about my personal life because most of my friends had gotten married and I was still single. So I decided to go on a week's vacation at a Club Med Village in the Paradise Island in the Bahamas. I took only one book with me to read on the beach while there. It was a book by John Powell, S. J. entitled "Happiness Is An Inside Job." It was there and from reading this book that God led me to understand that happiness does not depend on another person in my life, nor does happiness come from other people giving it to me. Happiness depends on me alone. Happiness is found deep within me. I had also started to understand what my mother's name "Felicidad," which when translated from Spanish to English is "Happiness," really means.

God is "Time." He allows doors to open and close so that we may see and then decide what is best for us in accord with His plans. In 1992, although it was difficult to leave the elegant city of Toronto that I had come to love, I moved back to the vibrant and diverse

33

immigrant city of Los Angeles. As I settled in again, at first I worked at an American Express travel office on the Westside. Spiritually, I was blessed to have found, and which I immediately joined, St. Monica Catholic Community in Santa Monica, California, under the dynamic leadership of Monsignor Lloyd Torgerson.[4] I then revived my friendships and contacts in California, including the Discalced Carmelite Friars of the California-Arizona Province who were delighted to learn of my return. They informed me of a forthcoming centenary celebration of the death of St. Thérèse that they were preparing for the years 1996 to 1997. I was asked if I would be willing to help them put together pilgrimages for this occasion. And so it happened. My travel ministry work in the United States was restored, and I named it "Littleways." With the Carmelite priests and nuns, we took busloads and busloads of pilgrims to Lisieux during those two years. In the years thereafter, I continued bringing pilgrims to Lisieux, and led many other pilgrimage programs to other holy places.

Yes, it is true, St. Thérèse did not have financial, professional, and even immigration concerns as I did. But she certainly watched over me, and helped me to persevere, by showering me with opportunities to learn even more about her "little way." And the opportunities she gave me were allowing me to go to the actual places of her birth and her life. As I organized pilgrimages and went to her hometown in Lisieux multiple times during this period, I came to understand her "little way" even more deeply.

Not Alone

And she didn't end it with that. She also showered me with other opportunities. She opened doors for me to work with other priests, nuns, and religious organizations. One of the major blessings I received was to be asked to work with someone I consider a living saint, the Most Reverend Joseph M. Sartoris (Bishop Joe), who was then Auxiliary Bishop in the Archdiocese of Los Angeles. With Bishop Joe, I took many pilgrims to Lourdes, Rome, the Holy Land, and other holy shrines all over the world. On several occasions I was in Rome and I was even privileged to touch and kiss the hand of St. Pope John Paul II. What beautiful blessings I received and how busy I had become!

But it was also at this time that I realized even more how important "prayer" is to be able to continue serving God's people. To find happiness in any state of life, it is important to pray, to be in communion always with the one and only true happiness. How to pray? Well, first of all, and most importantly is the Holy Sacrifice of the Mass. This is the ultimate of all prayers, for it is God Himself coming down to me, and I opening my heart and mind, and even my body to take Him in. I need Jesus in the Holy Eucharist in my life, and nothing can ever take His place. (In Chapter Six, I have written more about "Prayer" in the Carmelite and Ignatian traditions which I learned along my faith journey.)

And what about my dream of getting married? Well, I almost did in my late 40's, but now that I look back, I thank God, that I didn't. God had a different plan for me, and I was getting more and more immersed in His plan. However, it was not easy to realize and accept that being single was what He really wanted me to be, so I could continue my work for Him. But He helped me all along to realize this. Even after He called my Papa in 1996 and my aunt Tia Ayong in 1997 to join my Mommy in watching over me in heaven, God also gave me the Blessed Mother and St. Joseph as my intercessors. And besides the teachings of St. Thérèse, who had now been declared a Doctor of the Church, I also had the teachings of Mommy by which I was able to maintain strength through the vicissitudes of life.

Indeed, I was not alone! The Lord has never left me, even if at times I may have been the one who left Him alone.

Knock, Knock

It would not be right if I did not write something in this book about Mommy, with a prayer that readers can also learn from what I will share about her. She was someone who truly lived the "little way" of St. Thérèse. Mommy was a great example of what this childlike spirituality is all about, and a testimony of its relevance in the modern world of the 20th century.

My mother, Felicidad, was and will always be, the greatest person I will ever know in this world. She was a woman of faith, and firmly believed in God's Divine Providence throughout her 66 years on earth. Mommy dedicated her life to her family. Her mission was to give only the best to her six children. In wanting to do so, she suffered, but always with hope in God. One of the things she aspired to give us was a good Catholic education. I remember times when she pawned her jewelry, borrowed money, and begged the nuns and priests at school to extend the deadline for tuition payments. When everything seemed against her, she clung to novenas to the Infant Jesus of Prague until our Lord would prove to her what He said: *"Ask and you will receive; seek and you will find; knock and the door will be opened to you." (Luke 11:9).* My mother loved to go and help the Carmelite sisters in their convent in Quezon City where there was a beautiful chapel. Here she loved to pray, and when no one was around, she would literally, but respectfully go up to the Tabernacle and . . . knock!

She was determined to have all her children complete their education, not only in Catholic schools, but at the best ones in the city where we lived. She was also very ambitious, wanting us to achieve only the highest social standards. Mommy gave all she could so that we would be comfortable. She believed that if our lives could be just a little better than hers, she would have succeeded. But over and above all the material and social things she wanted for us, Mommy made sure to give us her love, faith, and trust in our Heavenly Father. She planted the seeds of her deep faith in all of us and watered them tenderly as we grew in years. Mommy loved roses and always asked St. Thérèse to send her these as signs. One thing she always taught me was to accept all the roses I receive in life along with their thorns, and to appreciate them together. I couldn't have one without the other.

A Rose for You

There was one special moment I had with this gentle lady that sums up what she taught me in life. I went with her to a weekday Mass, as I did often. There were only a handful of people in church one morning and there were a lot of choices where we could sit. We settled into a pew and the priest had just come out from the sacristy to the altar. All of a sudden the early morning sun came through the stained glass windows striking directly onto where we were.

I said, *"Let's move!"*

She replied, *"Bear a little."*

And so we stayed where we were. It was one of the most beautiful memories I have of my mother.

Thank you, Mommy, for teaching me to ask, seek, and "knock" so that the door can be opened for me. Thank you for teaching me the novena saying: *"O Little Thérèse of the Child Jesus, please pick for me a rose from the heavenly gardens and send it to me as a message of love."* And thank you for showing me how to accept "my rose" in life, my vocation to be single, so I can accomplish the work God wants me to do for His kingdom.

"Dear St. Thérèse,"
(Author to St. Thérèse)

Thank you for teaching me your "little way" so that I would not get lost in my many dreams, busy work, and material concerns. Like you, "I choose all," but help me always to remember what that "All" really means. What I want to thank you for even more is staying always by my side, showering me with roses, and then leading me always and only through the heart of Jesus to our Heavenly Father. Your "little way" is showing me that I am not alone!

"Write It Down!"
(Reader's Journey)

1. *What did you dream to be? Did your dreams come true?*

2. *What would you consider as the "starting line" in your career? Your vocation?*

3. *Can you describe a "crucible of trial" when you felt so alone (or lonely)? How did you deal with it?*

Chapter Three: The Tour Bus

"In the Footsteps of St. Thérèse"
(St. Thérèse's Journey)

"My life passed by tranquilly and happily. The affection with which I was surrounded at Les Buissonnets helped me grow. I was undoubtedly big enough now to commence the struggle, to commence knowing the world and the miseries with which it is filled." (SS, p. 49)

"Just as the sun shines simultaneously on the tall cedars and on each little flower as though it were alone on the earth, so Our Lord is occupied particularly with each soul as though there were no others like it. And just as in nature all the seasons are arranged in such a way as to make the humblest daisy bloom on a set day, in the same way, everything works out for the good of each soul." (SS, p. 14-15)

"A Littleways Journey"
(Author's Journey)

In this chapter, I recall the many lessons I learned about life while traveling on "the tour bus" with my Littleways pilgrims. I saw that life is but a journey, where fresh wonders reveal themselves each day, so long as I take the "little way." My profession, which I found to be most fulfilling when I treated it as a "travel ministry," helped me to understand how to deal with "saints and sinners" and "baggage" in my life journey. I also saw how necessary it was to find the right "companions" on the journey. Furthermore, it was a time for me to see even more clearly (though I was still not fully accepting it!) that the single state of life was the best one for me, if I were to deliver the work that God wanted me to undertake for Him. For how could I be on the road with my Littleways pilgrims with a husband and children back home waiting for me?

Saints & Sinners on The Tour Bus

First and foremost, in my role as Tour Director, I always needed to remind myself that I am not the only one who is on a journey. Everyone is traveling, and each one is at a different stage. One can walk faster than another, some can hardly walk, but whatever the circumstances are, all want to go somewhere. It would just be nice and easy if everyone was going in the same direction. But it does not always happen that way, even if we are on the same road, and even on the same tour bus. At times, the paths we take merge and we continue well on our way, but at other times, we find that we are going in opposite directions, or we must take a different route, or even take another bus. There are even times we may find that the road we are taking leads us to a dead end, and so we must go back and find our way again. The worst scenario would be if there is no room on another tour bus and we must find an alternate way. But as leader it was my task to make sure all my members got along and had a good time, and we all reached the destinations that were indicated in our itinerary.

The second thing I needed to recognize and accept was that each person is different. I could not change anyone, inasmuch as it is difficult enough to change my own self. It was necessary that I respect the different levels every member of the group was on, including mine, and I should not compare anyone to another. I always had to remember that every person has a perception, which is his or her reality, and more often than not, perception is greater than reality. Each person is unique; and God calls all of us individually by name.

The third thing for me to recognize was that, in order for me to give all the members of the group the "trip of a lifetime," I needed to look deeply to find where God exists in the story each of us was writing in our lives. It was the only way we could all enjoy our tour, and especially one another's company while traveling on the same tour bus. This was not always easy!

The differences among souls based upon the graces God bestows upon each was a situation well understood by young Thérèse. She wrote about it, in praise of God's merciful love:

"Oh my dear Mother! After so many graces can I not sing with the Psalmist: 'How GOOD is the Lord,

his MERCY endures forever!' It seems to me that if all creatures had received the same graces I received, God would be feared by none but would be loved to the point of folly; and through love, not through fear, no one would ever consent to cause Him any pain. I understand, however, that all souls cannot be the same, that it is necessary there be different types in order to honor each of God's perfections in a particular way. To me He has granted His infinite Mercy, and through it I contemplate and adore the other divine perfections! All of these perfections appear to be resplendent with love; even His Justice (and perhaps this even more so than the others) seems to me clothed in love. What a sweet joy it is to think that God is Just, i.e., that He takes into account our weakness, that He is perfectly aware of our fragile nature. What should I fear then? Ah! must not the infinitely just God, who deigns to pardon the faults of the prodigal son with so much kindness, be just also towards me who 'am with Him always'?" (SS, p. 180)

Before each tour group departed, I would hold a tour briefing, first, in order for the group members to meet one another, and also for me to lay the ground rules. One of my pet peeves was when one would come up to me with a list from someone's friend (or relative) who claimed to "know it all" because this person had been on a similar tour before. My answer would always be: *"This is your tour and you have saved a lot of money to go on your own tour. Leave your friend's tips and suggestions behind. It is good to be prepared, but please be open to what you will discover on your own."*

At the pre-departure briefing, I would give everyone a handout entitled "Know Before You Go." The opening line read like this:

Welcome to "A Littleways Journey!" You are just about to go on a tour which is not just any tour. You are going on a "pilgrimage." Webster defines "pilgrimage" as "a journey to some holy place ... the journey of human life."

41

Thus, I refer to my *Littleways* tours as "pilgrimages," and my tourists as "pilgrims."

When we returned, I would also organize a group reunion, to give an opportunity to share photos and memories, but most of all to reconnect with one another. It was always rewarding for me to see how many friendships had developed, and how many friends I myself had gained.   I saw how much fun those who followed my advice had experienced in not reliving someone else's tour but in making their own. No one can duplicate someone else's experience. Even for me who had been on many tours, every tour was different, even if the places visited were the same. What made it different each time was those with whom we traveled, and those we met along the way. Each pilgrimage I led made me a better person.   It was always my hope that every pilgrim who went with me also became a better person. I thank those who have been with me several times for allowing me to become a better person each time.

One of the hardest things to agree upon each day as we set out on the road was the temperature on the bus. Just as one would say it is too cold, another would say it is too hot. Moses wandered in the desert for 40 days and 40 nights. I recall the joke that the reason he got lost was because men do not like to ask for directions. What a journey that must have been. How did I manage to make a group happy when, I personally, was finding the temperature on the bus to be just fine? In looking back, I could not have conducted any tour without prayer. Prayer every day, lifting the day to our Lord, was the only way I was able to undertake each day on the pilgrimage with tactfulness, graciousness, and fun. It was only by the grace of God that I managed to make everyone happy, including myself.

Saints & Sinners

For me, "the wonders of the world" are the saints and sinners I found on my tour bus. I will start off by naming the biggest sinner – ME! But the good news is in realizing and accepting each time that I am not finished with myself. So also are the people that made my life difficult or those whom "I could not stand." They too are not yet finished with themselves. But I sympathize with those who also had to bear with me. St. Thérèse's insight into the human condition, as she experienced it herself within the walls of the Carmelite convent, helps me, not only on my tour bus, but everywhere I go when I am dealing with people. She reminds me that I am not alone in facing human frailties. God Himself is with me. This is what she wrote in loving our neighbor as ourselves:

> *"Ah! I understand now that charity consists in bearing with the faults of others, in not being surprised at their weakness, in being edified by the smallest acts of virtue we see them practice."* (SS, p. 220)

> *"Ah! Lord, I know you don't command the impossible. You know better than I do my weakness and imperfection; You know very well that never would I be able to love my Sisters as You love them, unless You, O my Jesus, loved them in me. It is because You wanted to give me this grace that You made Your new commandment. Oh! How I love this new commandment since it gives me the assurance that Your Will is to love in me all those You command me to love! . . . Yes, I feel it, when I am charitable, it is Jesus alone who is acting in me, and the more united I am to Him, the more also do I love my Sisters."* (SS, p. 221)

Being aware of the saying that "in a bunch, one will always find a rotten apple," every time I set out on a tour, I personally made it a point to carry with me St. Thérèse's autobiography, "Story of A Soul." Reading and re-reading page 222, which I quote below, always consoled me in knowing that even my patron saint had to work hard to be kind. Bearing with some people can be our purgatory here on earth! This is what she wrote:

> *"There is in the Community a Sister who has the faculty of displeasing me in everything, in her ways, her words, her character, everything seems very disagreeable to me. And still, she is a holy religious who must be very pleasing to God. Not wishing to give*

in to the natural antipathy I was experiencing, I told myself that charity must not consist in feelings but in works; then I set myself to doing for this Sister what I would do for the person I loved the most. Each time I met her I prayed to God for her, offering Him all her virtues and merits. I felt this was pleasing to Jesus, for there is no artist who doesn't love to receive praise for his works, and Jesus, the Artist of souls, is happy when we don't stop at the exterior, but, penetrating into the inner sanctuary where He chooses to dwell, we admire its beauty. I wasn't content simply with praying very much for this Sister who gave me so many struggles, but I took care to render her all the services possible, and when I was tempted to answer her back in a disagreeable manner, I was content with giving her my most friendly smile, and with changing the subject of the conversation, for the Imitation says: 'It is better to leave each one in his own opinion than to enter into arguments.'" (SS, p. 222)

Spiritual Leadership

There were some tours during which I would have wanted to separate the sheep from the goats. At times I even wished I could just leave the goats behind! But it was not for me to do so. As a leader, I always reminded myself that, like Jesus, I would not be able to please everyone. As one who was responsible for the welfare of the entire group, I found myself taking on contrasting virtues depending on situations that arose. At times I needed to compromise, and to be diplomatic or professional in how I would manage the day to day needs of the group in order to maintain camaraderie while touring. But there were also times when I found it necessary to take a firm stand, because the rule of the majority is not always the right solution. There were occasions when I had to be a "dictator" in order to protect my people from harm or danger, especially when I really knew what we would meet on the next stop, since I was the only one who had been there before. Oftentimes, I was fondly given the title "Reverend Mother" by my *Littleways* pilgrims, which I gladly accepted. One dear Carmelite priest with whom I planned a big program, had lovingly given me an honorary title: "Third Degree Carmelite!"

For three years, 1893 to 1896, St. Thérèse was assigned as "senior" or "angel," a role whereby she took charge helping a postulant to adapt to convent life. Although not given the title, she acted as the Novice Mistress. Thus, I could relate to her in my role as Tour Director to my *Littleways* pilgrims. These were "my spiritual children," even if most of them were older than I was. Like Thérèse, I could not have performed the task based upon my own merits. How, for instance, could I straighten out those who would "shop until they dropped," in spite of their having been briefed well that they have booked a pilgrimage, and not just a tour. Such "pilgrims" slowed down the whole group, and only became role models for "serving two masters." It was even more difficult to handle those who would make it known to me and to everyone else that they had "saved" a lot of money in order to go on their "once-in-a lifetime" trip, so it was their right to do as they pleased. My work was not easy, but I was consoled in reading my patroness' own experience as a guide because it was very similar to how I felt as I handled my *Littleways* pilgrims.

St. Thérèse's account of her role, (SS, p. 237-240), is something I find worth quoting below at length, because of its value not only to me as a Tour Director, but for any readers of this book who are in a position of spiritual leadership:

> *"I have recalled to you, dear Mother, the first work Jesus and you saw fit to accomplish through me. This was the prelude of those which were to be confided to me. When I was given the office of entering into the sanctuary of souls, I saw immediately that the task was beyond my strength. I threw myself into the arms of God as a little child and, hiding my face in His hair, I said: Lord, I am too little to nourish Your children; if You wish to give through me what is suitable for each, fill my little hand and without leaving Your arms or turning my head, I shall give Your treasures to the soul who will come and ask for nourishment. . ..*

Mother, from the moment I understood that it was impossible for me to do anything by myself, the task you imposed upon me no longer appeared difficult. I felt that the only thing necessary was to unite myself more and more to Jesus and that 'all these things will be given to you besides.' In fact, never was my hope mistaken, for God saw fit to fill my little hand as many times as it was necessary for nourishing the soul of my Sisters. I admit, dear Mother, that if I had depended in the least on my own strength, I would very soon have had to give up. From a distance it appears all roses to do good to souls, making them love God more and molding them according to one's personal views and ideas. At close range it is totally the contrary, the roses disappear; one feels that to do good is as impossible without God's help as to make the sun shine at night. One feels it absolutely necessary to forget one's likings, one's personal conceptions, and to guide souls along the road which Jesus has traced out for them without trying to make them walk one's own way. But this is still not the most difficult thing; what cost me more than anything else was to observe the faults and lightest imperfections and to wage a war to the death on these. I was going to say: unhappily for me! (but this would be cowardly), and so I say: happily for my Sisters, since the time I took my place in the arms of Jesus, I am like the watchman observing the enemy from the highest turret of a strong castle. Nothing escape my eyes; I am frequently astonished at seeing so clearly, and I find the Prophet Jonas very excusable when taking to flight rather than announcing the ruin of Nineveh. I would prefer a thousand times to receive reproofs than to give them to others; however, I feel it is necessary that this be a suffering for me, for, when we act according to nature, it is impossible for the soul being corrected to understand her faults; she sees only one thing: the Sister charged with directing me is angry, and all the blame is put on me who am filled with the best intentions. . ..

I told you, dear Mother, that I had learned very much when I was teaching others. I saw first of all that all souls have very much the same struggles to fight, but they differ so much from each other in other aspects that I have no trouble in understanding what Father Pichon was saying: 'There are really more differences among souls than there are among faces.' It is impossible to act with all in the same manner. With certain souls, I feel I must make myself little, not fearing to humble myself by admitting my own struggles and defects; seeing I have the same weaknesses as they, my little sisters in their turn admit their faults and rejoice because I understand them through experience. With others, on the contrary, I have seen that to do them any good I must be very firm and never go back on a decision once it is made. To abase oneself would not then be humility but weakness. God has given me the grace not to fear the battle; I must do my duty at all costs. . . .

Sometimes I can't help smiling interiorly when I witness the change that takes place from one day to the next; it is like magic almost. . . ." (SS, p. 237-240 – Fr. Almire Pichon, S.J. was Thérèse Spiritual Director.)

For me, these pages in the "Story of a Soul" have become my "guidelines" not only as a leader, but in my day-to-day encounters with people.

Spiritual Directors

And what about the priests who led the religious pilgrimages with me? At the outset, I always made it clear to my groups that while I was in charge of all the material operations of the program, the priest was in charge of the spiritual dimension. I justified the "separation of powers" as the only way I could provide my pilgrims with a pastoral dimension while on the pilgrimage. I was the Tour Director, while our accompanying priest was the Spiritual Director. I never allowed my priests to get bogged down with the technical operations. For the most part, I was blessed to have good tour chaplains (because I had chosen them). But there were a few times when I must admit that I was disappointed. On those few occasions, I reminded myself of the observations of my patron saint, St. Thérèse, who had experienced a pilgrimage tour herself. Of the priests who were on her month-long pilgrimage that she undertook with her father and her sister from France to Italy, she wrote:

> *"Having never lived close to them, I was not able to understand the principal aim of the Reform of Carmel. To pray for sinners attracted me, but to pray for the souls of priests whom I believed to be as pure as crystal seemed puzzling to me! I understood my vocation in Italy and that's not going too far in search of such useful knowledge. I lived in the company of many saintly priests for a month and I learned that, though their dignity raises them above the angels, they are nevertheless weak and fragile men."* (SS, p. 122)

So with her, as I learned this while on "my tour bus," I also made it my "vocation" to pray for priests.

In choosing spiritual director(s), St. Thérèse wrote a description that we can use as a guideline. She acknowledged this advice as coming from her patroness, St. Teresa of Avila who desired *"one combining knowledge and virtue."* (SS, p. 150) We also need to remember that ultimately, our spiritual director is "Someone" above any priest, clergy, or religious. This "Someone" is within us as St. Thérèse so beautifully stated: *"The way I was walking was so straight, so clear, I needed no other guide but Jesus. I compared directors to faithful mirrors, reflecting Jesus in souls, and I said that for me God was using no intermediary, He was acting directly!"* (SS, p.105). Later on during her first years in Carmel, she would refer to Jesus in this way: *"My Director."* (SS, p. 159)

Not to forget my drivers and my tour guides with whom I worked, and without whom I could not have gone anywhere, this brings me to another important lesson I learned. Although I made good use of God's gifts to me—strong organizational skills and attention to detail—I still recognized that I could not do it alone. I needed a good team to operate successful and meaningful programs. For this reason, I made sure I spent time and money to find the best working team to accompany me on all my *Littleways* journeys.

Baggage on The Journey

Besides recognizing that there can be both "saints" and "sinners" on my tour bus, I found a third "being" on my bus. This was the "baggage" that everyone carries! And this included not only the group members' baggage, but it included my very own. On tour, I saw how important it is to travel light, both in mind and body. It is imperative that everyone leave their "excess" baggage behind.

We begin with luggage. As Tour Director, it was one of my responsibilities to make sure we were not leaving anything behind when we moved on to our next destination. I would get annoyed when someone took out or added a suitcase without informing me ahead of time. I maintained an exact accounting of what everyone had for their baggage allowance. When we would leave a hotel, I counted all the pieces that I knew I was responsible for. When my numbers were not correct, I made everyone identify their luggage before I let them on the bus. Because it could mess up a day's schedule, I made it a point to remind everyone as often as I could that each one was allowed only one big suitcase to go in the baggage compartment. Anything over that needed to be their hand-carry, and this had to fit in the overhead rack inside the bus. But more importantly, I reminded them that for their carry-ons, they must be able to handle those themselves. My pilgrims were not to expect me or anyone else to carry their items for them. I also made them aware that when we reached our next hotel, I had a budget to pay the porters for one baggage per person. And even if they wanted to pay for an additional piece, the baggage compartment in the bus might not have had enough space. I would also tell them to be mindful of our bus driver who had to load and unload their suitcases at each of our stops.

My baggage responsibility as a Tour Director made me see that, as in real life, we need to take or keep with us only what is of real value in our lives. More importantly, we need to be mindful of how at times we can "dump" our baggage on others. So we need to constantly de-clutter, not only our homes and our surroundings of material things, but even our mind and spirit of negative thoughts and issues in order for us to be free and enjoy our journey of life. Carrying unnecessary "junk" only slows us down, and can make it impossible for us to reach our destination. And how much money and time do we spend hanging on to such matters in our lives, only to find out the answer to this question: Is it really necessary for our journey?

Baggage

In Mark 6:8-9, our Lord instructed his 12 disciples regarding how much they were to carry before he sent them out in pairs: *"He ordered them to take nothing for their journey except staff; no bread, no bag, no money in their belts; but to wear sandals and not to put on two tunics."* For how can we enjoy the sites we are to visit, appreciate the beauty of what is to come upon us, when we have a lot of baggage to worry about and pack, and re-pack each night? In Isaiah 65:17-19, we are instructed to free ourselves of such matters: *"For I am about to create new heavens and a new earth; the former things shall not be remembered or come to mind. But be glad and rejoice forever in what I am creating; for I am about to create Jerusalem as a joy, and its people as a delight. I will rejoice in Jerusalem, and delight in my people; no more shall the sound of weeping be heard in it, or the cry of distress."*

Our baggage includes more than what our eyes can see. What can be even heavier than material things are those that we do not see. And just as we are to be mindful of the baggage we carry for ourselves, we also need to recognize the baggage imposed on us by others, whether intentionally or unintentionally. This could be memories of cruel words said to us, relationships gone bad, opportunities lost, or pain inflicted on us by someone. Let these go! Isaiah reminds us that we can leave these with God and let Him lift such heavy weights away from us. For only in doing so can we really enjoy our tour of life.

In Luke 10:3-4, we read how Jesus again sent seventy-two men on their mission to go out in pairs to every town and place, and warned them also to be careful. He said: *"Go on your way. See, I am sending you out like lambs into the midst of wolves. Carry no purse, no bag, no sandals . . ."* Let us not forget that no matter how beautiful we

50

may see the world, even as we travel light, we still need to be careful and be discerning of the fact that wolves can dress in sheep's clothing even in what may seem the most holy of places as in our churches.

A Saint with Baggage on the Tour Bus

As I write about the baggage my group members take on the tours, I am reminded of one beautiful pilgrim who has been with me on several *Littleways* tours. She is the only one in the many thousands of group members for whom I always "closed my eyes" for her extra baggage. She is a very simple young lady who traveled with me to the Holy Land and Lourdes several times. Every year she would contact me to see where I was going next. She really did not care to go anywhere except to the Holy Land and Lourdes (and only with *Littleways*!) And she is someone I will always take with me anytime, regardless of her "excess" baggage.

She brought with her two suitcases each time. At first I wondered why she always had to have two; one was not very heavy, and the other, though not so heavy, had something she always guarded well. She explained to me that the light suitcase contained empty bottles, which when we reached Lourdes, she would fill up with holy water for the many friends she had promised to bring back Lourdes water. While she explained to me about the one suitcase, I still wondered about the other. I could not imagine that the other suitcase contained only her clothes as she dressed very simply every day. One evening, we were in Jerusalem and she did not feel very well. So I took some food to her room. Only then did I realize what was in the other suitcase.

She took with her, everywhere she went, big statues of St. Thérèse, St. Anthony, and St. Jude. She explained to me that as soon as we arrived at each hotel, the first thing she would do, would be to take out these three who she calls her "dream team" without whose protection she could not go anywhere. What purity of intention! For this reason, and because I have always known her to be very helpful to the needs of other pilgrims (a "saint" on "the tour bus"), I always allowed her to have two suitcases, even if I had to give her my very own baggage allowance.

God's love is the only baggage (or should I say "message") that we need to carry with us wherever we go.

Companions on The Journey

This beautiful lady's statues of her "dream team" with which she always traveled left me an image I will never forget. It taught me another important lesson I learned about life while I was on "the tour bus," that is, how important it is for us to have "companions" on our journey. But they need to be the right ones.

When Jesus sent out His disciples on the road, He sent them out in pairs. God realizes our need to be with friends we can enjoy on our life tours. These friends need to be in harmony with our personality, otherwise, we might as well go alone. Group tours are not for everyone. But those who go with a group, come back not only with many photos and souvenirs of places visited, they return home with newfound friends who can become lifetime companions of love and support on their life's journey. I personally have made many friends on *Littleways* tours. A special one who has become a dear friend joined a *Littleways* pilgrimage to Lisieux 20 years ago. This was in celebration of the 100th year anniversary of the death of my patron saint which I was commissioned to organize for the California-Arizona Province of the Discalced Carmelite Order. Since then, this dear friend has become like a sister, just as Céline was a sister to St. Thérèse.

Catholics have the Blessed Mother and the saints as "companions" on our faith journey. We look up to them as our role models. They were human beings who once lived in this world just like us. And not to forget our angels! On October 2, 2014, a day dedicated to Guardian Angels, Pope Francis' meditation was about their real presence in our lives, not just the fruit of our imagination.[5] He said that they are our traveling companion and that *"no one walks alone, and none of us can think he is alone: this companion is always there."* He even went on further to say that we need to ask ourselves this question:

> *"How is my relationship with my guardian angel? Do I listen to him? Do I bid him good day in the morning? Do I tell him: 'guard me while I sleep?' Do I speak with him? Do I ask his advice? Is he beside me?"*

He said that we must answer these questions in order to evaluate -

> ". . . *the relationship with this angel that the Lord*
> *has sent to guard me and to accompany me on the path,*
> *and who always beholds the face of the Father who is*
> *in heaven.*"

And even more real is the presence of Our Lord Jesus Christ within us. He is with us, forever in the "here" and "now," and wherever we go. Being single, the state of life that I found myself more and more in tune with as I did my travel ministry work, I found Him to be my best companion and the only One with whom I really need to travel. It is because of Him that I can go on the road with such enormous responsibilities. When I let myself be "little" and be guided and protected by Him, only then can I do the work our Heavenly Father wanted me to do for His people. Traveling on "the tour bus," I realized what St. Thérèse wrote and quoted from Luke 17:21:

> "*I understood and I know from experience that:*
> '*The kingdom of God is within you.*'" (SS, p. 179)

So how do we know who are the right companions for us on our journey? There is nothing more that can guarantee our relationships than when we focus these on Jesus. When we expect our family, friends, or anyone (and even anything!) in our lives to fulfill our needs that only God can fulfill, then we can become frustrated. It is like "promoting" roles to an unrealistic level so that disappointment will surely occur on both sides of the equation. And even our relationship with our Divine Master is affected, because then we reduce Him to what is not worthy of His name. We need to give all our relationships and attachments the right expectations. When companions on the journey are warmed enough by being focused on the love of Jesus, it leaves very little room for differences as to what temperature to maintain on the tour bus.

In The Footsteps of St. Thérèse

A Favorite Companion on The Journey

One very interesting thing I found out on one of my *Littleways* tours is that St. Thérèse is a favorite "companion on the journey." This is a result of a "contest of saints" I ran with one of my groups. We were just finishing a very long itinerary where we visited almost all the holy shrines of different Catholic saints in Europe. At our last group dinner, I held a party where I asked everyone to cast a vote for who was their favorite saint whose shrine we visited on the pilgrimage. St. Thérèse won by a landslide!

"Dear St. Thérèse,"
(Author to St. Thérèse)

Congratulations for winning the title of "the favorite saint!" What makes you a winner is because you are real. Even you had to bear with "rotten apples" in a small holy place - the Carmelite Convent where you lived. Thank you for teaching us how to bear with such matters by digging deeply to find Jesus in the core of such apples. Indeed, you are "the greatest saint of modern times." Please stay with us, especially when we feel alone in bearing other people's miseries, as well as our own. You understand that being on "the tour bus" is not as easy or exciting as it may seem to be.

"Write It Down!"
(Reader's Journey)

1. Who are the "saints" and "sinners" on your tour bus?

2. What baggage is the person(s) closest to you carrying? What is your own baggage?

3. Who is your favorite saint? Why? Have you read St. Therese's "Story of A Soul?"

Chapter Four: The Destination

"In the Footsteps of St. Thérèse
(St. Thérèse's Journey)

"How can a heart given over to the affection of creatures be intimately united with God? I feel this is not possible. Without having drunk the empoisoned cup of a too ardent love of creatures, I feel I cannot be mistaken. I have seen so many souls, seduced by this false light, fly like poor moths and burn their wings, and then return to the real and gentle light of Love that gives them new wings which are more brilliant and delicate, so that they can fly towards Jesus, that Divine Fire 'which burns without consuming.'" (SS, p. 83. She referred to St. John of the Cross's, *"Living Flame of Love"*)

"Doesn't Wisdom say: 'Life is like a ship that plows the restless waves and leaves after it no trace of its rapid passage'? When I think of these things, my soul is plunged into infinity, and it seems to me it already touches the eternal shore." (SS., p. 87. She referred to Wisdom 5:10)

"A Littleways Journey"
(Author's Journey)

In this Chapter, I have reached my 50's and time is clicking away toward realizing my dream of being married. As I continued to enjoy seeing the world and its many different cultures, I still continued to wonder if being single is really the way God wanted me to reach "my destination." There was also a question that, although I "sort of" always knew the answer, I did not seem to want to take the time, nor did I have the desire, to really think about it. This was the question: "What is my final destination?" I would ignore it, put it on the back burner, or even excuse myself by saying: "I am only young once. I have to enjoy my life!" It was as if "my destination" was something to think about only when I had nothing more to do in my life.

56

Where Art Thou, Oh Romeo?

Did St. Thérèse really know how it is to be alone so that singles can follow in her footsteps? Did she ever really experience loneliness? Her life may have seemed privileged and uncomplicated, but she understood that God allows pain in our lives only as we can bear it. After spending some happy years in *Les Buissonnets*, she started having fearful visions as losing her beloved father, which she could not even bear to think about. But she wrote:

> *"How good God really is! How He parcels out trials only according to the strength He gives us. Never, as I've said already, would I have been able to bear even the thought of the bitter pains the future held in store for me."* (SS, p. 47)

Little did she know that she would not only have fears of separation, but actual separation would come her way very soon. After St. Thérèse's mother died when she was only four years old, her sister Pauline became her second mother. But after only five years, Pauline decided to enter the Carmelite Convent. This was another "crucible of trial" which she described below:

> *I didn't know what Carmel was, but I understood that Pauline was going to leave me to enter a convent. I understood too, she would not wait for me and I was about to lose my second Mother! Ah! how can I express the anguish of my heart! In one instant, I understood what life was; until then, I had never seen it so sad; but it appeared to me in all its reality, and saw it was nothing but a continual suffering and separation. I shed bitter tears because I did not yet understand the joy of sacrifice. I was weak, so weak that I consider it a great grace to have been able to support a trial which seemed to be far above my strength!"* (SS, p. 58 – 59. This separation was so painful that she became very sick.)

Regarding her vocation, one might ask this question: Did she desire to enter Carmel only so she could be with her beloved sister Pauline, her second mother? Actually, little Thérèse was very sure of her vocation to the religious life, even before her real mother died. When she was only two years old, she had, in fact, already said that she wanted to be a religious. She wrote about this matter concerning her vocation and Pauline's entrance into Carmel:

> *"I felt this with so much force that there wasn't the least doubt in my heart; it was not the dream of a child led astray but the certitude of a divine call; I wanted to go to Carmel not for Pauline's sake but for Jesus alone. I was thinking very much about things which words could not express but which left a great peace in my soul."* (SS, p. 58)

Another question that might be asked, and most likely by singles who have not yet fully accepted their state of life, is this: Did St. Thérèse ever have any romantic interests? As I indicated several times earlier, I prefer to let her speak for herself by quoting directly from her book. Here's what she had to say about "love," and what she did not love:

> *"God gave me the grace of knowing the world just enough to despise it and separate myself from it."* (SS, p. 73)

This was how she described her "romance" with the only LOVE of her life, with whom she was physically united with for the first time, when she had her First Holy Communion at the age of 11.

> *"Ah! how sweet was that first kiss of Jesus! It was a kiss of love; I felt that I was loved, and I said: 'I love You, and I give myself to You forever!' There were no demands made, no struggles, no sacrifices; for a long time now Jesus and poor little Thérèse looked at and understood each other. That day, it was no longer simply a look, it was a fusion; they were no longer two,*

Thérèse had vanished as a drop of water is lost in the immensity of the ocean. Jesus alone remained; He was the Master, the King. Had not Thérèse asked Him to take away her liberty, for her liberty frightened her? She felt so feeble and fragile that she wanted to be united forever to the divine Strength!" (SS, p. 77)

Without a doubt, she had a "romance" and it was with the only One with Whom any romance can last forever. How could she have room for any other "man?"

The Little Way to God's Call

Even if St. Thérèse was so sure that God was calling her to be a Carmelite nun, this did not come easy for her. For one thing, she was very young (14 years old) when she realized and expressed her desire to enter the convent. She did not immediately get the permission of her father, her uncle, her aunt, and, most difficult of all, that of the ecclesiastical Superior of Lisieux Carmel, who would not consent to her entrance to the convent until she was twenty-one. But she was sure that God was calling her at her young age. She wrote about this to her sister, Pauline, who at first was the only one who really encouraged her, and whose very own vocation, made her see what Carmel would be like for her.

> *"Before 'resting in the shadow of him whom I desired,' I was to pass through many trials, but the divine call was so strong that had I been forced to pass through flames, I would have done it out of love for Jesus."* (SS, p. 106. She referred to the Canticle of Canticles, 2:3)

> *"If I hadn't had a vocation, I would have been stopped from the beginning, so many obstacles did I receive when trying to answer Jesus' call."* (SS, p. 106)

"There aren't many years to subtract because I wanted to be a religious since the dawn of my reason, and I wanted Carmel as soon as I knew about it. I find all the aspirations of my soul are fulfilled in this Order." (SS, p. 116. This was her reply to the Bishop of Lisieux who questioned how long she had desired to enter Carmel.)

Getting the necessary permission to realize her vocation was a battle she had to undergo wherein her emotions went uphill when she would obtain one person's approval, but downhill when she would be refused by another. She described her feelings as she went through these trials by relating it to nature. This is one quote that many of her devotees have learned from her as the "little way" of persistence and perseverance in listening to, and following God's call:

"I have noticed in all the serious circumstances of my life that nature always reflected the image of my soul. On days filled with tears the heavens cried alone with me; on days of joy the sun sent forth its joyful rays in profusion and the blue skies were not obscured by a single cloud." (SS, p. 110)

The young girl Thérèse was determined to do all within her power. She went (accompanied by her father who, by that time, was already very convinced of her vocation) to seek the permission of the Bishop of Bayeux, who had jurisdiction over Lisieux. She went with a persistent and persevering spirit in that, if the Bishop would not allow her wish, she would go directly to the Holy Father in Rome. And indeed, that was exactly what she had to do. She traveled to Rome with her father and her dear sister, Céline. Although they joined a group of other French pilgrims, her main objective was to obtain the Pope's permission to enter Carmel at her young age of 15. Off they went, and she received what she had to practically beg for, the Holy Father's reply in this way:

"Go . . . go . . . You will enter if God wills it!" (SS, p. 135)

St. Thérèse wrote about these trials as necessary means she needed to go through to "buy" her happiness. When she looked back at what she underwent, she had no regrets and described it this way:

> *"It is very true that 'love never finds impossibilities, because it believes everything is possible, everything is permitted.' It was surely only love of Jesus that could help me surmount these difficulties and the ones that followed, for it pleased Him to have me buy my vocation with great trials."* (SS, p. 114. She referred to The Imitation of Christ, III, 5:4)

> *"Today, when I am enjoying Carmel's solitude (resting in the shadow of him whom I have so ardently desired), I find I paid very little for my happiness, and would be ready to bear with even greater trials to acquire it if I still didn't have it!"* (SS, p. 114. She referred to the Canticle of Canticles: 2:3)

But in spite of her trials in listening to and following God's call, she was at peace. How powerful this is for us, especially for those of us who are single, and discerning God's will regarding our vocation. In following the footsteps of St. Thérèse, we know that God's call is in our desire, so long as our desire rests in Him, for only then can we be sure to find God's will.

> *"The more I approached the goal, the more I saw my affairs all mixed up. My soul was plunged into bitterness but into peace too, for I was seeking God's will."* (SS, p. 118)

In Search for Romeo

In my late 40's, nearly hitting the "50th milestone" of my life, I presumed I would marry a man I was seriously involved with at the time. Although it was not going very well, I was trying not to see the reality of the future I might have with him. In my mind I thought it would perhaps be my last chance to bear a child as my doctor had said that I still could if I did not wait any longer. But by the grace of God, He showed me that this man was still not the right man for me.

Although on the romantic side, things were not going well for me, my career got even busier. In addition to my *Littleways* work, I was offered a position at Carlson Marketing Worldwide, with good financial benefits, and even better, the requirements of the job made it possible for me to continue with *Littleways* while also at Carlson. As Travel Director at Carlson, I served top Fortune 500 company executives on travel programs that went all over the globe for events, meetings and conventions. What a wonderful opportunity for me to earn and finally to be able to save money for my retirement, which I could not do with the financial returns from my *Littleways* travel ministry alone. In addition, it allowed me to see even more exciting places and stay at the best hotels and resorts. I had a great team to work with too, and so I enjoyed it very much. Professionally, it was a perfect combination which allowed me to balance my travel ministry work with corporate and leisure travel work. It was no doubt, an opportunity "made in heaven."

This decade of my life can best be described in this way: Go, Go, Go. When I went, I didn't just "go," I didn't just walk, I ran. When I ran, I didn't just run, I rushed, rushed, rushed. Such was my life, exploring the world like it had no end. I would come home only to do my laundry. Much as I enjoyed my work and all the travel opportunities, as I globe-trotted, I also kept my eyes open to the possibility that I could still meet the man of my dreams, somewhere. It was as if I went the world over with some hope of still finding my Romeo!

Being Single

But this was not abnormal! My feelings were human, as explained in an article written by Rev. Ronald Rolheiser, OMI, entitled "The Single Life"[6] from where I gathered the following insights:

"The universe works in pairs. From the atoms to the human species, generativity is predicated on union with another. Happiness, it would seem, is also predicated on that.

So where does that leave singles and celibates? How can they be normal, generative and happy?

For many people living single and celibate, life can seem unfair. Everything, it seems, is set up for couples, while they are single. And that isn't the only problem. A further problem is that, too often, neither our churches nor our society give singles and celibates the symbolic-tools to understand their state in a life-giving way.

Consequently, single persons often feel like they're looking in at life from the outside, that they're abnormal, that they're missing something essential within life. Moreover, unlike married persons and vowed religious, few single persons feel that they have positively chosen their state of life. They feel it rather as an unfortunate conscription.

Few single persons feel easeful and accepting of their lot. Instead, they regard it as something temporary, something still to be overcome. Rarely does a single person, especially a younger person, see himself or herself growing old and dying single – and happy. Invariably the feeling is: This has to change. I didn't choose this! I can't see myself like this for the rest of my life!"

I can't think of any better explanation of the way I felt at this stage of my life regarding my still being single, than what Rev. Rolheiser wrote about so eloquently in this article. Though it was normal and understandable, he went further to caution about this:

"There are real dangers in feeling like this. First, there's the danger of "never fully and joyfully picking up one's life and seeing it as worthwhile, of never positively accepting what one is, of never accepting the

spirit that fits the life that one is actually living. As well, there's the danger of panicking and marrying simply because marriage is seen as a panacea with no real possibility of happiness outside of it."

He cited that even Thomas Merton, when reflecting on his celibate state, felt an *"irreparable loss"* which he had difficulty accepting. But the good news in Rev. Rolheiser's article was his bringing to light that *"paradoxically admitting this truth is the first step in beginning to live positively beyond those dangers."* He went further to explain that we are *"happy and whole"* when we have *"connection, community, family, friendship, affection, love, creativity, delight and generativity."* But the basis of happiness and wholeness in our lives is *"not on the basis of whether or not we sleep alone. The single celibate life offers its own opportunities for achieving these. God never closes one door without opening countless others."* I agree very much with Rev. Rolheiser's thought on this matter that "... *human sexuality and generativity are more than biological."*

Where Else To Go

A list of *Littleways* pilgrimages I planned, organized, and led can be found in "About Littleways" on page 103. As it would take up an entire book just by itself, I have not listed the many other trips I have undertaken as a corporate Travel Director. When at home in between tours, I also conducted local tours, events, meetings, and conventions for destination management companies in Southern California. With my family spread out all over the globe, personal trips and holidays make up another long list. One of my dear sisters wrote me a letter which I have kept as a lovely souvenir of those times of my life. She wrote: *"I get dizzy just keeping track of where you are going to be next!"* During those years, my address was simply – "The World!"

Each time I went on an airplane, train, ship, or bus, my prayer was always Psalm 121:1-8 which I found in a bookmark, and which I stuck in my book of St. Thérèse together with my sister's letter. I call this "My Traveling Prayer." I enjoyed traveling and did not feel alone.

I lift up my eyes to the hills—from where will my help come?
My help comes from the LORD, who made heaven and earth.
He will not let your foot be moved; he who keeps you will not slumber.
He who keeps Israel will neither slumber nor sleep.
The LORD is your keeper; the LORD is your shade at your right hand.
The sun shall not strike you by day, nor the moon by night.
The LORD will keep you from all evil; he will keep your life.
The LORD will keep your going out and your coming in from
this time on and forevermore.

Lourdes and Lisieux

Very high on my personal list of favorite places to visit were Lourdes and Lisieux. In both locations, I also worked as a volunteer on two separate occasions in 1994. I went to Lourdes during the summer, first intending to practice my French. But more than the language, I found myself practicing my eyes, my ears, and my heart with compassion. For me, Lourdes is the happiest place on earth (not Disneyland!) because this is where so many sick people travel long distances to seek God's loving mercy for a cure. But whether they received what they came for or not, it was the place where I saw countless pilgrims experience overwhelming joy in knowing our Lady is watching over them with her mantle of protection, and that Jesus journeys with them in their sickness and pain.

In Lisieux, I went during the fall of 1994, basically to observe how the ceremonies surrounding St. Thérèse's feast were celebrated in preparation for my big assignment from the Discalced Carmelites for 1996 -1997 to celebrate the 100th anniversary of her death. This was a time I will remember for the rest of my life. I went and just charged all my needs on my credit card. But I knew and believed strongly that God wanted me to go and learn everything possible so that I would be able to continue planning the *Littleways* pilgrimages that were already on my books. It was a time when I indeed learned a great deal. But more than anything else, it was when I truly learned and understood the "littleness" of my patron saint. It was also at this time that the Catholic world was preparing for St. Thérèse to be declared a "Doctor" of the Church. This experience made me see that indeed, her "little way" is a way we can all take on our journey to our final destination.

How well I could relate to what she wrote about when she had the opportunity to make a pilgrimage to the Eternal City. Although her intention was to seek the Holy Father's approval to enter Carmel at age 15, she learned many things about life on her trip, just as I did on all my tours and travel. She wrote:

> *"Ah! what a trip that was! It taught me more than long years of studies; it showed me the vanity of everything that happens and that 'everything is affliction of spirit under the sun.' However, I saw some very beautiful things: I contemplated all the marvels of art and religion; above all, I trod the same soil as did the holy apostles, the soil bedewed with the blood of martyrs. And my soul grew through contact with holy things."* (SS, p. 121. She referred to Ecclesiastes 2:11)

That said and realized, where else can I go? Thus, I took many more pilgrims to the holy places in the following years.

Just Want To Be Home

I enjoyed every bit of my globetrotting profession. But gradually, my interests began to turn toward home and just "staying put." Having gone almost everywhere, there were not many more destinations I really cared to visit. But there was another "tour" God seemed to be calling me to undertake. Only later would I find that it was the "journey of my soul."

Whenever I was on the road with my groups, I was "high," truly enjoying every moment of it. But as time went on, each time I returned home I began to feel lonely. "Where, oh where art thou, my Romeo?" Am I missing a lot for not concentrating on finding you? Should I just find another job that would allow me to build on fellowship and community at "home" rather than on the road? And yet, there was this silence that I also enjoyed when I was home alone, re-charging myself before I went on another trip. It was more than "silence." It was "solitude"—that "peace" and "quiet," as the dictionary tries to describe it.

Those short times I spent at home were times for rest and for finding myself again. But each time, I found myself gradually changing. Whenever I was home resting, my perspective was becoming much like what St. Thérèse experienced when she was in the attic at *Les Buissonnets*, which became *"a world for me"* as she described for herself: *"It was this room I loved to stay alone for hours on end to study and meditate before the beautiful view which stretched out before my eyes."* (SS, p. 91). It began to be harder and harder for me to leave my "home." I started savoring my "solitude."

This brings to mind one unforgettable incident I had when I was so eager and in a hurry to get home, much as I enjoyed the traveling. Each of my *Littleways* pilgrimages was marked with unexpected and sometimes hilarious events. On one of these trips, which included Lourdes and Fatima, I couldn't resist buying a bottle of Porto, the national wine of Portugal, to bring home and enjoy. I loved buying the different wines and liquor from places we visited such as Sambuca from Italy, Calvados from Lisieux, and Cana Wine from the Holy Land.

So there was my treasured bottle of Porto, packed carefully in my luggage alongside my laptop, my portable printer, my camera and other important items. Our flight home included a stopover at the international terminal at JFK Airport in New York with a connecting flight to Los Angeles. Well, wouldn't you know it, my bottle of Porto broke, filling my suitcase and of course everything in it! At first I thought "Oh no" but in the end all I could do was laugh. I'll never forget, my fellow pilgrims and I on our hands and knees, in front of onlookers, spreading out everything from my suitcase onto the terminal floor at JFK in vain attempts at drying out my computer and the other contents of my baggage. Of course, the smell of Porto filled the entire terminal. I think we used up all the paper towels we could find in the restrooms as well as clothing items my fellow pilgrims pulled out of their bags to sop up the mess. In the end, everyone's luggage smelled like Porto for the remainder of our trip. Eventually I was able to "rescue" my laptop, but my group members and I will never forget that smell of Porto.

To this day, it reminds me of what turned out to be a hilarious event at JFK. And with it, all I remember was—I just wanted to get home then and get some rest!

"Dear St. Thérèse,"
(Author to St. Thérèse)

How wonderful that you found your Romeo very early in your life, and you did not have to search the world over. How complicated I can make my life at times by going on a "merry-go-round." Yet God, in His loving mercy, allows me to take such a ride so I can test my heart's desire. But He wants only to show me that He is all Who really matters—He is "My Romeo" and He is "My Destination." His call is in my desire, and anything without Him will only make me "dizzy." Thank you for teaching me to be persistent and persevering in listening to His call, although at times I pretend not to hear Him. Thank you for showing me my "little room" where I can rest and just be with Him. Who says I am alone?

"Write It Down!"
(Reader's Journey)

1. *Where have you traveled? What is your favorite destination? Why?*

2. *What do you think the difference is between "silence" and "solitude"?*

3. *When have you started NOT feeling alone, even when you were alone?*

Chapter Five: The Market Roundup

"In the Footsteps of St. Thérèse
(St. Thérèse's Journey)

"I find myself at a period in my life when I can cast a glance upon the past; my soul has matured in the crucible of exterior and interior trials. And now, like a flower strengthened by the storm, I can raise my head and see the words of Psalm 22 realized in me: 'The Lord is my Shepherd, I shall not want; he makes me lie down in green pastures. He leads me beside still waters; he restores my soul. Even though I walk through the valley of the shadow of death, I fear no evil; for thou are with me . . .' To me the Lord has always been 'merciful and good, slow to anger and abounding in steadfast love.' Psalm 102: v.8" (SS, p. 15)

"A Littleways Journey"
(Author's Journey)

As I approached my 60's, and the bulls and bears in the economy tumbled over one another, I had a chance to re-charge and explore a new purpose in life. With so much time on my hands, I then found myself quieting down which led me to attend to another journey. But this time, it was no one else's tour but mine. It was a different kind; it was the "journey of my soul."

69

Recession to Recovery

And so I did get home! But to my surprise, God gave me a chance to be home more often than I expected, and much more than I really wanted. It was a time that left a mark not only on my life, but on the rest of the world. This economic period caught everyone either "dead" or "alive." The bulls and bears in the economy tumbled over one another. In my personal timeline, it covered seven years—2007 to 2014—that made up a period of my life which I refer to as "my market roundup." This was a very difficult period and posed big challenges for me because I was also approaching my 60's. But it actually became a time of significant blessings, and I see now that God allowed this in my life so that I could take some rest from being a Tour and Travel Director. He permitted this time for me so that I could give Him the chance to be "My Director" in another kind of journey that He wanted me to undertake.

Recession

According to the U.S. National Bureau of Economic Research, an 18-month period from December 2007 to June 2009, can now be defined as: "Recession." A sharp increase in oil and food prices made what was already a bad financial situation become even more difficult for Americans and most of the rest of the world. According to Wikipedia, this crisis began due to losses from sub-prime loans in 2007 and over-inflated asset prices. A major panic broke out on the inter-bank loan market in September 2008. Housing prices declined, and many large and well-established investment and commercial banks in the United States and Europe suffered huge losses and even faced bankruptcy, resulting in massive public financial assistance.

In May 2006, at the height of the housing market and just before the period of economic recession began, I decided to sell my townhouse. It was a beautiful unit in a prime location in Marina del Rey, California. Though at first I was hesitant to let it go, I made a move that I can now give credit only to God's gentle divine intervention in my life. If I had not "obeyed" and instead hung on to it, I would have burst with the bubble. I then invested my earnings in a well-thought-out portfolio of stocks, bonds, and mutual funds.

My corporate travel career income was also at its peak up to the end of 2007, and just before the recession began. Many years of working very long hours with Carlson Marketing Worldwide were paying off well. It was a rewarding job with full benefits that included a company-matched 401K that I was putting away for my retirement. I was earning more than my basic needs and sustaining a comfortable lifestyle.

"What does the market tell me would be wise to do next?"

"What do I want to do next?"

These were two questions I asked myself after I sold the townhouse and settled down in a leased apartment. It was a nice unit overlooking the marina where I enjoyed looking out my window, and where I also would regularly watch CNBC and enjoy seeing my investments rocket skyward. But as I looked out at the heavens each time, there seemed to be a third question hovering above me:

"What does God want me to do next?"

Asking this question does not seem to have a place in this day and age. Financial analysts and planners have a formula or a prediction in regards to every move in the market. Then, in a blink of an eye, the economic world started tumbling down. My investments and what I was saving for retirement, started diminishing in value, and my travel work and ministry was also slowing down. I remember September of 2008. The crisis happened right around my birthday when I also reached another milestone in my life. The Dow Jones, and just about everything else, took a deep turn.

"What should I do next?"

The more I asked myself this, the more I found that I needed to re-shape my query to –

"Why is God allowing a recession at this time of my life?"

My work for over three decades had involved planning, organizing, and leading individuals, families, special interest groups, corporate executives and VIP's on their tours and travel. I was circling from one end of the globe to the other. I was enjoying every place there was to see, meeting many people of different cultures and traditions. I was not only earning a living; I was also having a ball. My youngest sister used to describe my work energy this way:

"You don't only walk; you are always running!"

Indeed, that was my pace.

But all of a sudden I found myself neither walking nor running. I had no choice but to slow down, pull back, and withdraw just as the economic world was doing. At times I even panicked and worried:

"How will I pay my rent?"

"How will I sustain my life?"

My anxieties were compounded by the fact that I was single. I had no husband, nor children to take care of me. I spent a lot of energy worrying as I sent out my résumé. I did find some jobs, here and there, but none that was stable enough on which to build a new career. The age factor was also starting to creep up on me. As the slump went on, I started to wonder:

"Does God still have a purpose for my life?"

The Little Way in the 21st Century

It was a very difficult and crucial period in my life. I started feeling alone. This was a time when I must confess that, as much as I loved and followed my patron saint, St. Thérèse, I wondered if she could understand what I was going through at that time. She did not have to worry about such things as "aging" or "recession." She died at 24; that did not even give her enough time in her life to think of or worry about "retirement." Did she even think of who was going to take care of her when she would be old and gray? She lived with a community where she was well-taken-care-of during her illness. She had no worries when she became ill, except to die. She knew she would be buried well and would be remembered beyond the grave, at least by her sisters and her Carmelite community. What about me and singles like me who never marry and have no children? Of course I have my loving family, my siblings, and my nephews and nieces. But they have lives of their own, and they have their parents to think of, and to take care of first before having time to look after me. I wondered how relevant my patron saint would still be to me at my age, and in the 21st century with the problems I was facing.

Well, what I love about St. Thérèse is that whenever I talk to her this way, she always points me to Jesus. One day during Adoration, I felt her presence. But she was just kneeling next to me, with her finger pointing toward Jesus. It was as if the Blessed Mother and Mommy were also there with her next to me. And all three were kneeling down in front of the Blessed Sacrament with me, and all three of them were pointing out Jesus to me. And then I found myself saying to Jesus:

> *"You have taken care of me all this time, why will you not take care of me even more now and when I need you most?"*

And then it really made sense to me what St. Thérèse wrote and which I followed:

> *"Prayer is an aspiration of the heart, it is a simple glance directed to heaven, it is a cry of gratitude and love in the midst of trial as well as joy."* (SS, p. 242)

Recovery

On March 7, 2014, The Los Angeles Times reported in its Market Roundup column that, "Jobless data help lift most stocks." About this time, my personal life also rounded up a very difficult period, from late 2007 to early 2014, which I can now look back on. It was as if during those seven years I was traveling to a place where I saw "bulls and bears" fluctuating in the arena every day. Well, it was on this "trip" that I decided instead to be a "lamb." What I have come to see and believe is that—yes, I am single but I am not alone!

> *"You open your hand, satisfying the desire of every living thing."*
> *(Psalm 145:16)*

I could not have survived this period of my life without prayer. Where do I go from here? I realized that I can go EVERYWHERE, but I cannot go ANYWHERE without PRAYER. And furthermore, I have seen that I will never be alone because -

"The LORD is my shepherd, I shall not want." (Psalm 23:1)

The Bride

During "The Market Roundup" period of my life, there was one specific moment that I can point to when I finally came to terms and accepted my single vocation of my own free will. It was sometime in May of 2011. I had my apartment blessed by a priest and I had a few friends over for dinner for the occasion. After blessing every nook and corner of my home, the priest also blessed me with a "wish" that I find the right husband soon. But before he could complete his prayer, I stopped him and I said:

"Oh no, Father! I don't want a husband!" My friends looked at me, and could not believe what they were hearing. I continued to say *"I mean it. I am really very happy the way I am."*

Then the priest said: *"What if the next 10 years of your life with a husband will be the happiest in your life?"*

My reply to him was this: *"I am happy now. I do not want to get married!"*

From 2011 to 2013, with my travel work and ministry still being slow, God blessed me with a part-time job at Loyola Marymount University. This Jesuit-run university is located just a few minutes from where I live, and where for nearly two decades I went to daily noon Mass every time I was home between tours. I was a familiar face on campus, just for being a neighbor who went to worship there regularly. One day during the recession years, as I found myself going to daily Mass more often than usual, a nun who works at Campus Ministry asked if I would be interested in helping out as Wedding Coordinator, because the priest in charge needed help, and she wanted to recommend me. The university has a beautiful chapel, a very much sought-after venue for alumni and staff to have their Catholic wedding ceremonies. Oh what a wonderful ministry that turned out to be. It also became a grace for me personally to confirm the vocation God planned for me.

During those three years, I met such wonderful couples for whom I helped plan their wedding ceremonies. I found myself with a task that God wanted me to undertake, that is, helping new couples to keep the right perspective as they go through planning what was probably the biggest event of their lives together. God used me as His instrument for these lovely couples to remind them, amidst the many stresses they were going through, that what they were really preparing for was not only a big wedding party, but a holy sacrament that they will receive for life. The couples were very appreciative of my role, and at the same time, they also helped to confirm my single vocation. While I have much respect and appreciation for the married state of life, for me, those three years helped me see what I "naughtily" described as my "job description." I coined this phrase to identify my role, but it was an "honest-to-goodness" description of how I started to feel about my single vocation. I say of myself that I am this:

Always a bridesmaid, never a bride . . . living happily ever after!

I mean this sincerely and without a bit of sarcasm nor any misgivings on my part as I found and embraced my vocation. I say this without looking any less nor demeaning at the two other beautiful states of life, those of being married or the religious life. We are asked to just follow what God wants us to be. This is what makes the state of life we are in to be lived: "happily ever after." St. Paul explains this so eloquently in his advice to all states of life in 1 Corinthians 7:25-35:

> *"Now concerning virgins, I have no command of the Lord, but I give my opinion as one who by the Lord's mercy is trustworthy. I think that, in view of the impending crisis, it is well for you to remain as you are. Are you bound to a wife? Do not seek to be free. Are you free from a wife? Do not seek a wife. But if*

you marry, you do not sin, and if a virgin marries, she does not sin. Yet those who marry will experience distress in this life, and I would spare you that. I mean, brothers and sisters, the appointed time has grown short; from now on, let even those who have wives be as though they hand none, and those who mourn as though they were not mourning, and those who rejoice as though they were not rejoicing, and those who buy as though they had no possessions, and those who deal with the world as though they had no dealings with it. For the present form of this world is passing away.

I want you to be free from anxieties. The unmarried man is anxious about the affairs of the Lord, how to please the Lord; but the married man is anxious about the affairs of the world, how to please his wife, and his interests are divided. And the unmarried woman and the virgin are anxious about the affairs of the Lord, so that they may be holy in body and spirit; but the married woman is anxious about the affairs of the world, how to please her husband. I say this for your own benefit, not to put any restraint upon you, but to promote good order and unhindered devotion to the Lord."

The Bridegroom

I took St. Paul's advice to mean for me that when I accepted my single state, I also decided NOT to be alone for the rest of my life. In accepting the vocation God intended for me, it was like I walked down the aisle, as couples do on their wedding day. I let Jesus take me as His bride, and it was with Him that I made my vow of commitment. Finally, I heard the angels in chorus singing for me Richard Wagner's song, "Here Comes The Bride." and my heart was filled with joy! I also heard this:

"Look! Here is the bridegroom! Come out to meet him."
(Matthew 25:6)

After four decades of searching, and even trekking the world over to find my Prince Charming, I finally found "Him" and "He" became "My Bridegroom." The sentence I rehearsed with all my wedding couples also applied to me, as I accepted Jesus to be my life partner:

> *I_____, take you, _____ to be my wife/husband. I promise to be true to you in good times and in bad, in sickness and in health. I will love you and honor you all the days of my life.*

I realized these vows were very similar to the promises God made to humanity from the dawn of creation, and how I experienced him in the "journey of my soul." In every joy as well as trial I encountered in life from the day I was born, and especially during "my market roundup," God was always there drawing Himself to me in covenants of love. He has never left me alone.

Once at a Christmas midnight Mass I attended while visiting my sister in Vancouver, Canada, I listened to the homily of a priest I did not know, but whose reflection finally made sense to me. He explained that the true meaning of Christmas can be gathered from these wedding vows. Christmas is God giving His Son Jesus to be like us in our humanity, "a fulfillment of His promise to be true to us in good times and in bad, in sickness and in health, loving and honoring us all the days of His life." Indeed, God wedded me to His being – to Jesus, "My Bridegroom!"

How do I describe "My Bridegroom?" This isn't easy because He is beyond words. In trying to talk about Him, I prefer instead to follow what St. Thérèse said: *"I felt it was more valuable to speak to Him than to speak about Him . . ."* (SS, p. 87). The best I can do is to hope that I can please "My Bridegroom" in being the "valiant woman" that He deserves, as written in Proverbs: 31:10-13; 19-20; 30-31:

"A capable wife who can find? She is far more precious than jewels. The heart of her husband trusts in her, and he will have no lack of gain. She does him good, and not harm, all the days of her life. She seeks wool and flax, and works with willing hands.

She puts her hands to the distaff, and her hands hold the spindle. She opens her hand to the poor, and reaches out her hands to the needy.

Charm is deceitful, and beauty is vain, but a woman who fears the LORD is to be praised. Give her a share in the fruit of her hands, and let her works praise her in the city gates."

And so it is! I got married to Jesus, "My Bridegroom" during "The Market Roundup." Where do I go from here? It was also during this time that I started to follow a very strong calling to write about my life with Jesus, as a single person, in the hope that I could help those who may be single and still feel alone.

"Dear St. Thérèse,"
(Author to St. Thérèse)

Oh yes, how relevant you still are in the 21st century, and to any age or state of life, for that matter! What makes you timeless is your childlike faith and trust in God's love. I have advanced in age now so much further than what you lived on this earth. But what still makes you a great model for me to follow is that you showed me life just the way it is. You succeeded in following God's purpose for your short life, which is to show the world that we do not need more than God's love. Your love of Jesus is so contagious that you make me also desire to love only Him. Thank you for showing me how to satisfy the aspirations of my heart by looking up to heaven and lifting all my needs to Him who always loves me.

"Write It Down!"
(Reader's Journey)

1. How have you been affected by economic recession, or anything similar to it? What did you do? How did you overcome it?

2. Have you ever felt so alone? What, where, or who did you turn to?

3. What experiences of St. Thérèse are similar to your own life experiences?

Chapter Six: How To Be Single But Not Alone

"In the Footsteps of St. Thérèse
(St. Thérèse's Journey)

"I was very fond of the countryside, flowers, birds, etc. . . . I preferred to go alone and sit down on the grass bedecked with flowers, and then my thoughts became very profound indeed! Without knowing what it was to meditate, my soul was absorbed in real prayer. I listened to distant sounds, the murmuring of the wind, etc. At times, the indistinct notes of some military music reached me where I was, filling my heart with a sweet melancholy. Earth then seemed to be a place of exile and I could dream only of heaven." (SS, p. 37)

"A Littleways Journey"
(Author's Journey)

In this chapter, I have reached the present. As I try to "live happily ever after," St. Thérèse keeps true to her promise of sending "a shower of roses." I find that I need to constantly spark my relationship with Jesus in "the language of prayer," most of all by uniting myself with Him in the Holy Eucharist as often and as regularly as I can. As I continue to follow in the footsteps of St. Thérèse, I had opportunities to learn from other saints, and those whom my patron saint followed during her lifetime. I also learned more about Carmelite spirituality, as well as Ignatian spirituality. Then, following these traditions, the "little way" of St. Thérèse, and based upon my personal experiences, I have put together, "The Ten Commandments For How To Be Single But Not Alone."

A Shower of Roses

St. Thérèse, The Little Flower, the saint of the modern world (and the 21st century!), is known for a promise she made as she was dying, that she will let fall from heaven "a shower of roses." Many devotees ask for her intercession and request a sign indicating whether their petition will be granted, or at times of making a decision, ask for her gentle prodding on which way to go. The sign usually asked for is that of a rose. This is symbolic, but also real, when one looks deeply into what life on earth is all about. Her promise to send roses was intended not only for us to have the mere pleasure of having a beautiful flower. Her promise also consists in her example of how to receive it, and how to enjoy it fully even with its thorns. A few months before her death, she stated clearly her intention:

> *"I feel that my mission is about to begin, my mission of making others love God as I love Him, my mission of teaching my little way to souls. If God answers my requests, my heaven will be spent on earth up until the end of the world. Yes, I want to spend my heaven in doing good on earth."* (SS, p. 263)

For me, her "little way" has become my inspiration on how to live my chosen single vocation. All states of life, even if one has answered the right call, do not really end in "living happily ever after" like the fairy tales we read in our childhood. Being single, just like being married, or being a religious, involves working on a relationship in a lifetime journey of faith. St. Thérèse's *"little way"* is about *"child-like trust and gentle love."* It is about *"simplicity and love in the ordinary events of life."* It is about how *"our All-Loving God hears and responds to our needs, according to the mysterious ways of His Love."*[7]

Singles in Spiritual Leadership

When one has found Jesus in a loving relationship, the person is also led to give of self in service. When one comes to this realization and serves the church or community, it can be said that Christian maturity has been reached. Such involvement is remarkable not only for the recipients of service, but also for the individual who serves. It is a mutual giving and receiving, flowing from the Sacred Heart of Jesus, and therefore bringing joy to those who give, as well as to those who receive. For anyone embarking on such a role, it is necessary to be in the right frame of mind, or else it is probably better to not be of service at all. One must serve in the light of "servant leadership" which was well explained by Henri J.M. Nouwen in his book, "In the Name of Jesus." He describes this type of leadership at page 63:

> *". . . a leadership that is not modeled on the power games of the world, but in the servant-leader Jesus, who came to give his life for the salvation of many."*

Without a doubt, what Nouwen describes is very much within the context of the "little way." One is better off to not get involved in ministry or spiritual leadership if it is meant only to fill in the void of one's "lonely" times, to run away from some personal need, or even worse, to be on center stage in order to gain attention. St. Thérèse wrote about this as follows:

> *"It is true that in reading certain tales of chivalry, I didn't always understand the realities of life; but soon God made me feel that true glory is that which will last eternally, and to reach it, it isn't necessary to perform striking works but to hide oneself and practice virtue in such a way that the left hand knows not what the right is doing."* (SS, p. 72. See also Matthew 6:3)

A word of caution for singles! In as much as we need to be pure in our intentions when we embark on service, it is also important to be aware of another matter! In her book, entitled "Celebrating the Single Life," Susan Annette Muto explains how not surprisingly, single persons can be found in the forefront of spiritual leadership, but how easily singles can be envied, by virtue of not having family or communal concerns to deal with, thus having more time to devote in the pursuit of creativity and community service. She wrote on page 72:

"By contrast, it should come as no surprise to singles if their pursuit of professional excellence arouses envy in some colleagues. One simply has to live with this reality. If it results in a feeling of loneliness, that too has to be expected. To think one can be a single, dedicated, skilled professional without occasionally arousing envy or feeling lonely would be naïve. Having encountered these two experiences frequently in my own life, I've come to accept them as normal challenges of the single state."[8]

Herein, I cite a firsthand experience I encountered as a single person, and how I took it as "a shower of roses" and dealt with it in the "little way" as best I could. This became for me a grace of growing even closer to "My Bridegroom" and realizing that even if I am single, I am not alone! Jesus is always there for me, bearing my pain, carrying my crosses with me, and making me fall in love with Him even more.

Although I was a frequent volunteer at church ministries, there occurred a leadership role for which I did not volunteer. In fact, I had to be persuaded to accept it. It was during this time, and in this capacity of spiritual leadership, that I personally experienced extreme jealousy from a particular individual. Sad to say, it happened in a small Catholic community. It was in some ways similar to what St. Thérèse experienced with students at the Benedictine Abbey, which was her boarding school. This is what she narrated, and to which I could closely relate:

"But now I had to come in contact with students who were much different, distracted, and unwilling to observe regulations, and this made me very unhappy. I had a happy disposition, but I didn't know how to enter into games of my age-level; often during the recreations, I leaned against a tree and studied my companions at a distance, giving myself up to serious reflections!" (SS, p.81)

In my role of spiritual leadership, I encountered from one individual, jealousy, distraction, and an unwillingness to "observe regulations" and this made me exceedingly unhappy, despite my "happy disposition" (see above quotation from St. Thérèse). The individual in question was not accepting of my leadership role and she retaliated in ways that were very hurtful. It was an experience not easily forgotten, but in retrospect, it did bring me down on my knees in prayer. This whole experience actually became an opportunity for spiritual growth for me as I tried my best to regard the offending person with compassion and lifted her up in prayer, often re-counting words referred to by Mother Teresa of Calcutta: *"Be kinder than necessary, for everyone you meet is fighting some kind of battle."*[9] Of course, I also tried to follow the example of St. Thérèse in staying "little." In meditating on God's love before the Blessed Sacrament, I found myself thanking Him that what I had to bear was only "a rose thorn" and not "a crown of thorns," because Jesus had already done the latter for me.

During this difficult and prolonged period, I thanked God for giving me the grace to follow Pope Francis' Daily Meditations where I discovered something he had to say about such human situations. The Holy Father explained that in the heart of a person affected by jealousy and envy, two things come out as a result: 1) The envious and jealous person is a bitter person who always looks at what someone else has that he or she does not have. This leads to bitterness that spreads throughout the whole community. 2) When someone cannot stand to see that someone else has something he wishes for himself, he puts the other person down, so that he may be a bit higher up. The tool used to do this is "gossip" which divides and destroys the community. Rumors are the weapons of the devil.[10]

Our Holy Father was describing my situation exactly as it was happening. Every time I felt the sting of this envy, I realized that my patron saint was showing me that the "little way" is not only "the little things we do," but "the little things we forgive." And so I came out the "winner" in the end because as a single person, even if I did not have a human shoulder to cry on, I learned the "language of prayer;" that is, I learned to talk it ALL with Jesus. Oh, what peace and joy I found!

The Language of Prayer

Now I realize that during times in the past when I felt alone being single, it was mainly because I was not communicating with Someone who was already and always with me.

What is "Prayer?" Simply put, for me prayer is "talking to," "being with," and "centering" my heart on Someone who is deep within me. It is placing myself faithfully and regularly in the presence of an Almighty who does not only exist up there in heaven, but who is always with me, and to whom I can tell ALL! He is also the only One I really need to "listen to." Most of all, it is keeping myself united with Him in the Holy Eucharist. St. Thérèse described this union with Jesus when we receive Him in Holy Communion in such a way that one would not want to miss an opportunity to receive Him as often as one could. She wrote:

> *"It is not to remain in a golden ciborium that He comes to us each day from heaven; it's to find another heaven, infinitely more dear to Him than the first: the heaven of our soul, made to His image, the living temple of the adorable Trinity!"* (SS, p. 104)

My profession and my vocation gave me the opportunity to live in four countries and be fluent in four languages. But it was the "language of prayer" that I found to be the most important for me to master so that I would be able to fulfill the work God wanted me to do as a single person. In this section, I also recall the many opportunities God gave me to learn from other saints and their spiritual traditions, such as the Carmelite and Ignatian spiritualities. I am still learning these and have a long way to go in developing my prayer life for my faith journey.

Ignatian Spirituality

There is no doubt that St. Thérèse also learned from St. Ignatius of Loyola when she became a Carmelite. In following her footsteps, the Ignatian tradition, which began in the early half of the 16th century, provides us with "spiritual exercises" to take along the "little way."

The best way I can explain Ignatian Spirituality is by citing a homily given by Most Reverend Gordon D. Bennett, S.J. (Bishop Gordon) on February 22, 2015 at the Sacred Heart Chapel at Loyola Marymount University. His homily moved me immensely. I took notes and summarized it, and immediately went to see him to confirm what he had actually said and how I had understood him. He said it was indeed correct, and gave me his permission to share it in this book.

It was the First Sunday of Lent, and the Gospel was about Jesus going out into the desert to pray for 40 days (Mark 1:12-15). He also referred to Viktor Frankl's "Man's Search for Meaning," which I mentioned in Chapter Two as one of my favorite books in school.

Bishop Gordon reminded us that Jesus, in His humanity, needed to find the "why" of what He was about to undergo. Jesus went to the desert to find His meaning. To find it, He needed to go into solitary prayer. It was in the desert that Jesus discovered His "why." But Bishop Gordon cautioned us. He pointed out that it was also in the desert that Jesus was tempted by the devil. Like Jesus, even if we have found our "why's," there is a constant pull that we will experience, just as Jesus did. There are two voices that will prompt us on a daily basis. Thus, he said, is the importance of prayer.

In Ignatian Spirituality, I learned from "The Spiritual Exercises of St. Ignatius" about "The Awareness Examen" which is recommended that we do regularly. This is my favorite explanation of what this examination is all about, which I quote from Bishop Gordon: *"A way of reminding ourselves of both who we are and whose we are. It is a way we can do what we can to live into God's grace, the grace that is always present, always available, always good, and always victorious."*

Bishop Gordon concluded his homily by reminding us that we can go through our "how" and any kind of "how" if we have found our "why." Having found the answer to both questions, he told us not to be afraid to give up our "default pattern" because God will save us from the power of sin and will reconcile us to Himself. The Holy Spirit will bring everything to completion, all we need to do is say "Yes."

Needless to say, this tradition is very much present in the "little way" of St. Thérèse.

Carmelite Spirituality

As St. Thérèse was a Carmelite, I will start off explaining Carmelite spirituality by quoting what St. Thérèse wrote about "prayer." This is the tradition that she grew into and walked along in her faith journey.

> *"One day, one of my teachers at the Abbey asked me what I did on my free afternoons when I was alone. I told her I went behind my bed in an empty space which was there, and that it was easy to close myself in with my bed-curtain and that 'I thought.' 'But what do you think about?' she asked. 'I think about God, about life, about ETERNITY . . . I think!' The good religious laughed heartily at me, and later on she loved reminding me of the time when I thought, asking me if I was still thinking. I understand now that I was making mental prayer without knowing it and that God was already instructing me in secret."* (SS, p. 74-75)

The one I love most in how St. Thérèse described the way she prayed, and which I find myself following every day, is this:

> *"I was thinking things over in my bed (for it was there I made my profound meditations, and, contrary to the bride in the Canticles, I always found my Beloved there) . . . "* (SS, p. 71)

The Carmelite tradition dates back to the Western hermits in the 12th century who settled on Mount Carmel, overlooking the plain of Galilee, and who grouped themselves around a small chapel dedicated to Our Lady, imitating Elijah, as can be read in 1 Kings 18:19-46. But today, the Carmelite tradition is known for how it was reformed in the 16th century by St. Teresa of Avila and St. John of the Cross. It is their charism and teachings that were followed by St. Thérèse. In fact, she mentioned a little incident that occurred when she was five years old, and she was at Mass with her father. This shows that even from her childhood, she had looked up to St. Teresa of Avila, after whom she was named:

> *"The first I did understand and which touched me deeply was a sermon on the Passion preached by Father Ducellier and since then I've understood all the others. When the preacher spoke about St. Teresa, Papa leaned over and whispered: 'Listen carefully, little Queen, he's talking about your Patroness.' I did listen carefully . . ."* (SS, p. 42)

On March 28, 2015, on the anniversary of the birthday of St. Teresa of Avila, Pope Francis described her as "primarily a teacher of prayer." Her teachings still apply today, 500 years later! As St. Teresa of Avila said, "Prayer" consists simply in having *"a relationship of friendship . . . with He, who we know, loves us."* (Life, 8. 5).[11]

In praying, St. Teresa said that the important thing is not to think much, but to love much. It is nothing else but an intimate sharing between friends. And it means taking time frequently to be alone with our Friend. During prayer, she said, *"Just look at Him."* At a Lenten daily reflection put together by the Discalced Carmelite Friars which I found on their website, my dear friend, Fr. Donald Kinney, O.C.D. showed how other Carmelite saints followed St. Teresa's example and "just look at Him."[12] Here is Fr. Donald's reflection for March 11, 2015, which gives a good description of what Carmelite Spirituality is all about:

> *St. John of the Cross writes beautifully of this quest in The Spiritual Canticle (10-11):*
> > *May my eyes behold you,*
> > *because you are their light*
> > *and I would open them to you alone.*

Reveal your presence,
and may the vision of your beauty be my death;
for the sickness of love is not cured
except by your very presence and image.

St. Thérèse of the Child Jesus of the Holy Face is another who yearned for the vision of the face of Christ. For example, in her "Oblation to Merciful Love," this is what she longs for during her life on earth. This is what she longs for her Heaven to be: "I want, O my Beloved, with each beat of my heart to renew this offering to You an infinite number of times, until the shadows having disappeared I may be able to tell You of my Love in an Eternal Face to Face." (Story of A Soul, p. 277).

Blessed Elizabeth of the Trinity, in her famous prayer "O Trinity Whom I adore," exclaims, "I want to gaze on You always and remain in Your great light."

St. Teresa of Los Andes writes, "You can always look at Him. That sight will bring you peace, if you are disturbed or exalted. It will fortify you, if you are cast down; it will bring you recollection, if you are dissipated." (L 137).

St. Teresa Benedicta of the Cross writes, "To stand before the face of the living God—that is our vocation... Elijah stands before God's face because all of his love belongs to the Lord." ("On the History and Spirit of Carmel", The Hidden Life, pp., 1,2).

So St. Teresa's phrase, "Just look at Him," is a whole way of life, a great adventure. Saints down through the ages have lived it, and so can we.

(Fr. Donald Kinney, O.C.D.)

"Prayer" is the impact in my life of St. Teresa of Avila, who was also the patron saint of my school, which I wrote about in Chapter One, but which I needed to re-learn in "how to be single but not alone." My patron saint, St. Thérèse of Lisieux called St. Teresa her "mother." I am so blessed to realize by following their Carmelite spirituality that:

"Prayer" is how I can be . . . "single but not alone."
"Prayer" is how I can live . . . "happily ever after."

For as St. Teresa of Avila, the great saint of the 16th century whose 500th birth anniversary is being celebrated in 2015, the year that I am writing this book, said:

"Let nothing disturb you. Let nothing frighten you.
All things are passing. God never changes.
Patience obtains all things.
Nothing is wanting to those who possess God.
God alone suffices."

(St. Teresa of Avila)

How much I have grown from the way I used to pray, which I wrote about in the first chapters of this book. Thank you, dear Saints, for helping me to learn "the language of prayer," and furthermore, for letting me see how much more room there is for me to grow. I hope someday, I can make it up there to heaven with you all!

The Ten Commandments
For How To Be Single But Not Alone

After finally accepting my vocation as a single person, I wanted to have a set of guidelines with which I could continue on the path of my life journey. When I planned my *Littleways* pilgrimages, I mapped out where and how I would take my pilgrims. I would do extensive research on the best, safest, and most enjoyable ways to get my groups from one point to another. However, for my own life journey, I could not find much research material, books or programs for singles who have never married, and who wish to enjoy their chosen vocation. So now, the only thing on which I can base the following Ten Commandments is my own experience and with the guidance of the Holy Spirit.

I have put together these commandments, first and foremost, for me to follow. But herein I offer these—as well as my life's experiences—to anyone who, like me, wishes to remain on this course. Thus, the "Thou" I address below refers both "to me" and "the other." "The Ten Commandments For How To Be Single But Not Alone" is my set of guidelines on "how to live happily ever after" with My Bridegroom Jesus. It is a relationship of love that needs to grow every day, as He leads me to the heavenly garden where only there can be found roses with no thorns.

The Ten Commandments For How To Be Single But Not Alone

1. ***Thou shalt look at life as a process where fresh wonders reveal themselves on each day's journey.*** *Nothing is forever. The only constant in life is change. Jesus alone will stay with me forever.*

2. ***Thou shalt start your day saying to Jesus, "The Lord is my Shepherd, there is nothing I shall want."*** *My "Spiritual Director" is Jesus, and only Jesus! It is He Who I walk hand-in-hand with throughout my day.*

3. ***Thou shalt tell Him every day, and several times a day, in "the language of prayer" how much you love Him.*** *Reading, writing, or talking about Jesus cannot take the place of "BEING" with Him. And there is nothing more intimate than when I take Him in the Holy Eucharist and let Him dwell inside of me.*

4. ***Thou shalt regard your family, friendships, and work highly, but in their right priorities without ceasing to love and to be committed to them.*** *But I must remember that all my attachments become stronger only when I anchor them on Jesus.*

5. **Thou shalt not feel sorry for yourself when you see married couples enjoying their children and grandchildren.** *My life is becoming full when I am in solitude with Jesus. He allows me this time so I can give birth to a legacy which He has intended for me. If I let Him, my "descendants" will be as numerous as the stars.*

6. **Thou shalt not try to please everyone in everything you do.** *Remember that, even if I am doing something for Jesus, I may not be able to please everyone. Perception is greater than reality. Even Jesus could not please everyone. What is most important is that I please Jesus.*

7. **Thou shalt live one day at a time, enjoying one moment at a time, and accepting hardship as the pathway to peace.** *Remember "The Serenity Prayer," that there are things I cannot change. It is only with the help of Jesus that I can change the things that need to be changed. Tightly holding Jesus' hands, I must take this sinful world as it is, not as I would have it, and without having to be one like it. I need to be true to my name, and my married name is "Jesus."*

8. **Thou shalt do your best to forgive anything that hurt you and forget as much of it as you can.** *Whatever I can't do, I need only to let go and let Jesus do it for me. What is most important is my desire to forgive. I can let the heart of Jesus love those who are difficult to love, for after all, in being married to Jesus, my heart beats as one with His.*

9. **Thou shalt live your day taking care of your spirit, your mind, and your body.** *These are gifts that help me to live a long life of being single but not alone. I must remember to do my "Awareness Examen" every day and to maintain my spiritual journal. I will also*

remember that gratitude is my best attitude in all circumstances I meet throughout the day.

10. **Thou shalt "dream big to be little . . . be little to dream big."** *I will remember what St. Thérèse, the saint of spiritual childhood taught: "It is the little things we do out of love that charm the heart of the good God." I will present all my dreams to Jesus, and together we will present these to our Heavenly Father, trusting what He said, "Ask and you will receive, seek and you will find, knock and it shall be opened to you." And in "dreaming," I will dream not only for myself, but I will remember also . . . "those who have not!"*

This is **"How To Be Single But Not Alone."** It is with no doubt that I cannot do it alone. It is only with Jesus that I can be single but not alone. He is the only One who makes it possible. As St. Thérèse said:

"Oh my God, You surpassed all my expectation.
I want only to sing of Your Mercies."
(SS, p. 208)

"Dear St. Thérèse,"
(Author to St. Thérèse)

"St. Thérèse, help me to always believe as you did, in God's great love for me, so that I might imitate your 'Little Way' each day."

(From "My Novena Rose Prayer," Society of the Little Flower)

"Write It Down!"
(Reader's Journey)

1. *When do you feel most alone?*

2. *How do you pray?*

3. *How do you feel with how you pray?*

Chapter Seven: Conclusion

"In the Footsteps of St. Thérèse
(St. Thérèse's Journey)

"I understood that if the Church had a body composed of different members, the most necessary and most noble of all could not be lacking to it, and so I understood that the Church had a Heart and that this Heart was BURNING WITH LOVE. I understood it was Love alone that made the Church's members act, that if Love ever became extinct, apostles would not preach the Gospel and martyrs would not shed their blood. . . ." (SS, p. 194)

"A Littleways Journey"
(Author's Journey)

What makes St. Thérèse who lived in the 19th century relevant in the 21st century? Can singles who feel alone, and even those who no longer feel alone, really follow in her footsteps? Can her "little way" also apply to other states of life? Can she be a role model for any age or gender? In this chapter, I conclude YES without any doubt!

And one does not even have to be Catholic to appreciate her teachings.

In The Footsteps of St. Thérèse

The "Story of A Soul" has become St. Thérèse's legacy to the world and several of our Holy Fathers have recognized her *"little way."* In 1921 Pope Benedict XV promulgated the practice of her virtue *"to all the faithful of every nation, no matter what their age, sex, or state of life."* In 1923 Pope Pius XI, who beatified and canonized her as a saint, described her *"little way"* as a way *"to arrive at the kingdom of heaven."* Her teaching continued to be relevant throughout the 20th century. In 1997 St. Pope John Paul II declared her a Doctor of the Church. Currently, Pope Francis not only continues to recommend her as a role model, he sets himself up as an example of one who also seeks her intercession in his undertakings. Following in her footsteps is in union with Holy Mother Church, who supports that her teachings be passed on to the next generation(s).

The "little way" of St. Thérèse can be seen well in how she dealt with two insignificant incidents in her daily life. In summarizing how and why she handled these the way she did, she wrote: *"My dear Mother, you can see that I am a very little soul and that I can offer God only very little things."* (SS, p. 250). What she experienced are similar occurrences we can find in our lives, no matter what state of life we are in, whatever our age, gender, or wherever in the world we live. It is heartwarming to read her accounts as quoted below:

> *"The practice of charity, as I have said, dear Mother, was not always so sweet for me, and to prove it to you I am going to recount certain little struggles which will certainly make you smile. For a long time at evening meditation, I was placed in front of a Sister who had a strange habit and I think many lights because she rarely used a book during meditation. This is what I noticed: as soon as this Sister arrived, she began making a strange little noise which resembled the noise one would make when rubbing two shells, one against the other. I was the only one to notice it because I had extremely sensitive hearing (too much so at times). Mother, it would be impossible for*

me to tell you how much this little noise wearied me. I had a great desire to turn my head and stare at the culprit who was very certainly unaware of her 'click.' This would be the only way of enlightening her. However, in the bottom of my heart I felt it was much better to suffer this out of love for God and not to cause the Sister any pain. I remained calm, therefore, and tried to unite myself to God and to forget the little noise. Everything was useless. I felt the perspiration inundate me, and I was obliged simply to make a prayer of suffering; however, while suffering, I searched for a way of doing it without annoyance and with peace and joy, at least in the interior of my soul. I tried to love the little noise which was so displeasing; instead of trying not to hear it (impossible), I paid close attention so as to hear it well, as though it were a delightful concert, and my prayer (which was not the Prayer of Quiet) was spent in offering this concert to Jesus.

Another time, I was in the laundry doing the washing in front of a Sister who was throwing dirty water into my face every time she lifted the handkerchiefs to her bench; my first reaction was to draw back and wipe my face to show the sister who was sprinkling me that she would do me a favor to be more careful. But I immediately thought I would be very foolish to refuse these treasures which were being given to me so generously, and I took care not to show my struggle. I put forth all my efforts to desire receiving very much of this dirty water, and was so successful that in the end I had really taken a liking to this kind of aspersion, and I promised myself to return another time to this nice place where one received so many treasures." (SS, p. 249-250)

What makes St. Thérèse who lived in the 19th century relevant in the 21st century? In fact, one will see that she was relevant before her time, in our present time, and she will remain relevant in centuries to come.   What makes this so is that her teachings on "spiritual childhood" are well grounded in Holy Scriptures.   Here are some quotations from the Old and New Testaments upon which her "little way" has been based:

Isaiah 66:12-13
For thus says the LORD; I will extend prosperity to her like a river, and the wealth of the nations like an overflowing stream; and you shall nurse and be carried on her arm, and dandled on her knees.   As a mother comforts her child, so I will comfort you; you shall be comforted in Jerusalem.

Psalm 131:1-3
O LORD, my heart is not lifted up, my eyes are not raised too high; I do not occupy myself with things too great and too marvelous for me.   But I have calmed and quieted my soul, like a weaned child with its mother; my soul is like the weaned child that is with me.   O Israel, hope in the LORD from this time on and forevermore.

Matthew 11:25-26
At that time Jesus said, "I thank you, Father, Lord of heaven and earth, because you have hidden these things from the wise and the intelligent and have revealed them to infants; yes, Father, for such was your gracious will."

Mark 10:13-16
People were bringing little children to him in order that he might touch them; and the disciples spoke sternly to them.   But when Jesus saw this, he was indignant and said to them, "Let the little children come to me; do not stop them; for it is to such as these that the kingdom of God belongs.   Truly I tell you, whoever does not receive the kingdom of God as a little child will never enter it."   And he took them up in his arms, laid his hands on them, and blessed them.

98

Unlike most of us, at a very young age, St. Thérèse was sure of her vocation to be a religious, a cloistered Carmelite nun. She had been in the convent and was nearing her last days on earth when she wrote about ALL vocations. This is the summary of her life, and the answer to why walking **"In the Footsteps of St. Thérèse"** is a way to follow in one's faith journey. She wrote:

> *". . . I understood that LOVE COMPRISED ALL VOCATIONS, THAT LOVE WAS EVERYTHING, THAT IT EMBRACED ALL TIMES AND PLACES . . . IN A WORD, THAT IT WAS ETERNAL!! . . . O Jesus, my Love . . . my vocation, at last I have found it . . . MY VOCATION IS LOVE! Yes, I have found my place in the Church and it is You, O my God, who have given me this place; in the heart of the Church, my Mother, I shall be Love. Thus I shall Be everything, and thus my dream will be realized."* (SS, p. 194)

(St. Thérèse, The Little Flower)

Yes, ALL of us can follow in the footsteps of St. Thérèse: singles who feel alone; those who no longer feel alone; those in other states of life; those of any age or gender; and of all generations. This is because when we follow in St. Thérèse's footsteps, the One Who we really follow is Jesus, the Son of the Most High, who was sent to us, to show us how to live.

Thus, is following "In The Footsteps of St. Thérèse" and *"How To Be Single but Not Alone"* in which I humbly call *"A Littleways Journey."*

"Dear St. Thérèse,"
(Author to St. Thérèse)

"Little Flower, give me your childlike faith, to see the Face of God in the people and experiences of my life, and to love God with full confidence. St. Thérèse, my Carmelite Sister, I will fulfill your plea 'to be made known everywhere' and I will continue to lead others to Jesus through you. Amen."

(From "Miraculous Invocation to St. Thérèse" - Society of the Little Flower)

"Write It Down!"
(Reader's Journey)

1. What is the impact of the "little way" of St. Thérèse in your life?

2. From your life experiences and in your own "little way," what can you share with the world as a legacy?

3. How will you share this legacy?

Acknowledgments

A special dedication and acknowledgment to "my Céline," Nina R. Messina, for checking every single thought and spirit that went into this book. I am blessed to have you as my Carmelite "soul-sister" in the reality of this world. Thank you for being my "sister," just as Céline was a sister to St. Thérèse.

A special dedication and acknowledgment to Sr. Joanna Carroll, CSJ. Thank you for the opportunities you opened up to me which enabled me to also learn about Ignatian Spirituality. And thank you for reminding me that I need to take time writing this book because it is an art that I must enjoy.

A special dedication and acknowledgment to Jessica La Rocca, my former graduate assistant. She is one "millennial" who has listened to "my story" from the early stages of my writing it, through to its completion. This lovely and intelligent young professional lady, who from the age of 21 (when she obtained her Master's degree in Psychology), through the age of 26 (at the time of my completing this book) has "therapized" me with her friendship, by always keeping me aware of the needs of the next generation(s).

I acknowledge with gratitude, the thousands of Littleways pilgrims I have been privileged to take to holy places, on cruises, on fun-tours, or just on get-aways. I also remember several VIPs and corporate executives I accompanied on their meetings and conventions. Allowing me to lead you on your "trips of a lifetime" has helped me see that . . . life is but a journey, where fresh wonders reveal themselves each day.

About the Author

Teresita A. Ong is fondly called "Terri" (or "Titay" by her family and those she grew up with). Born and raised in the Philippines, having lived in four countries, and fluent in four languages, she brings to the literary world valuable international experience with multi-cultural insights. She earned a B.A. in Foreign Service at St. Theresa's College, Quezon City, Philippines, an M.A. in Asian Studies from the University of the Philippines, and was a research scholar at the International Christian University in Tokyo, Japan. Her career spanned over three decades in the travel industry: as an airline employee; as a travel office manager; as a travel director for top Fortune 500 executives; and as a tour organizer/tour director, leading Catholic pilgrimages, meetings, conventions, and international celebrations.

Reflecting on her journeys, Terri felt a very strong calling to extend her "travel ministry" to a "writing and speaking ministry." Terri is a certified travel professional by the International Tour Management Institute, Inc. She is an active member of the Catholic Writers Guild. She is also a speaker, certified as a "Competent Communicator" by Toastmasters International. She belongs to the "Speakers By the Sea Club" in Playa del Rey, CA, and consistently wins awards for inspirational speeches. She is a lector at her parish, St. Monica's Church, and at Loyola Marymount University. She assists as a volunteer at the Sacred Heart Retreat House in Alhambra, California, where she has given a talk on "Single Life" at a "Day of Discernment." Terri has also given a talk on the impact of St. Teresa of Avila in her prayer life as a single person at "A Symposium and Celebration" of the 500th anniversary of the saint's birth in 2015, organized by the Discalced Carmelite Friars of the California-Arizona Province of St. Joseph, at El Carmelo Retreat House in Redlands, California.

Terri lives in Marina del Rey, California, her home state for over 30 years. To know more about her work, refer to: www.littleways.com; www.facebook.com/Teresita.Terri.Ong; or – E-mail: showerofroses@littleways.com.

About "Littleways"

Formerly known as "Orient Pacific Services Inc." and "OPSI Golden Pilgrimage Tours and Travel" when it began 1981, *Littleways* is managed and operated by Teresita "Terri" Ong. *Littleways* is devoted to special interest tours and travel related services. *Littleways* is a pioneer in organizing Catholic pilgrimages. It was in 1994, that it adopted its current name, *Littleways,* which best describes what everyone experiences on its tours. Besides the sites one visits, traveling with *Littleways* makes one appreciate that life is indeed a beautiful journey where "little ways" count.

The following are Catholic pilgrimages that have been organized by Teresita:

- Pilgrimage to the Holy Land for St. Mark's Parish, Venice, CA, March 2008.
- Pilgrimage to France (Paris - Lisieux - Lourdes) with Carmelite Gilbert Levario, September 2005.
- "The Road to Rome" with Rev. Fr. Reginald McSweeney, O.C.D., August 2005.
- Mexico Pilgrimage with Terri, March 2005.
- French Vineyards & Vistas - A Cruise Tour on the Viking Burgundy with Terri, September 2004.
- Pilgrimage to France (Paris - Lisieux - Lourdes) with Rev. Fr. Reginald McSweeney O.C.D., August 2004.
- Alaska Cruise Tour with Rev. Fr. Freddie Chua, July 2003.
- Mexico Pilgrimage with Bishop Joseph M. Sartoris, January 2003.
- "A Pilgrimage to Our Lady's Shrine in Knock" & "Leisurely Ireland" to celebrate the golden jubilee of Rev. Fr. Reginald McSweeney, O.C.D.'s ordination, July 2002.
- "Gems of the Baltic Sea" - A Scandinavian Holiday with Bishop Joseph M. Sartoris, July, 2002.
- "Treasures of China & Yangtze River Cruise" with Bishop Joseph M. Sartoris, August 2001.
- "In the Footsteps of St. Thérèse" & "A Marian Celebration" with Rev. Fr. Reginald McSweeney, O.C.D., October, 1998.

- Holy Year Pilgrimage to the Holy Land with Bishop Joseph M. Sartoris, September 2000.
- "Opening of the Holy Door" - Rome Pilgrimage, December 1999.
- "In the Heart of Europe" – Austria, Germany, Holland, & Rhine River Cruise with Bishop Joseph M. Sartoris, October, 1999.
- "An Easter Celebration in Lourdes and Paris" with Bishop Joseph M. Sartoris, April, 1999.
- "A Lenten Retreat to the Holy Land & Rome" with Carmelite Gilbert Levario and Deacons, March, 1999.
- "In the Footsteps of St. Thérèse" & "A Marian Celebration" with Rev. Fr. William Fenton, O.C.D., September 1998.
- "A Retreat to the Holy Land & Rome" with Rev. Fr. Reginald McSweeney, O.C.D., September, 1998.
- "A Pilgrimage to Italy and Cruising Italian Style" with Bishop Joseph M. Sartoris, June 1998.
- "A Lenten Retreat to the Holy Land & Rome" with Rev. Fr. Jan Lundberg, O.C.D., March 1998.
- "In the Footsteps of St. Thérèse" (Celebrating the Centenary Year of the Death of St. Thérèse) - Program I & II, sponsored by the Discalced Carmelite Friars, California-Arizona Province of St. Joseph, September - October 1996 and 1997.
- Pilgrimage with Bishop Joseph M. Sartoris to the Holy Land, Jordan, & Egypt, June 1997.
- Lourdes & Fatima (+ Paris, Nevers, & Lisbon) with Rev. Fr. (Dr.) Flavian, C.M.F., May 1997.
- Holy Land + Paris & Lisieux with Carmelite Gilbert Levario, March, 1997.
- Leisurely Ireland & Pilgrimage with Rev. Fr. Patrick Sugrue, O.C.D., July 1996.
- Pilgrimage to Lourdes with Bishop Joseph M. Sartoris, Archdiocese of Los Angeles, June 1996.
- Pilgrimage to Our Lady of Guadalupe, Mexico with Rev. Fr. (Dr.) Flavian, C.M.F., May 1996.
- Holy Land & Marian Shrines with Rev. Fr. Adam Civu, Notre Dame of Jerusalem Center, and Rev. Fr. Bernard Perkins, O.C.D., March, 1996.

- Rome, Holy Land, & Paris with Marian Shrines, September 1995, led by Rev. Fr. (Dr.) Flavian, C.M.F. and Rev. Fr. Adam Civu, Notre Dame of Jerusalem Center.
- Easter Week in the Holy Land, April 1995, led by Rev. Fr. Patrick Sugrue, O.C.D.
- Carmelite Marian Pilgrimage, September 1994, led by Rev. Fr. Patrick Sugrue, O.C.D.
- Marian Pilgrimage, July 1988, from various parishes in Southern and Northern California, led by Rev. Fr. Mateo Hicarte and Rev. Fr. John McSweeney.
- Canonization Pilgrimage in honor of Lorenzo Ruiz, first Filipino Saint, October 1987, sponsored by the Filipino Priests Fellowship of Southern California.
- Holy Land & Europe Pilgrimage, September 1987, led by Rev. Fr. Stephen Watson, O.C.D., Superior, El Carmelo Retreat House, Redlands, CA.
- Marian Pilgrimage, June 1987, led by Deacon Ralph Bovy, St. Julie Billiart Church, Newbury Park.
- Holy Week in the Holy Land, Spring 1986, with Rev. Fr. Michael Buckley, O.C.D., Provincial, Discalced Carmelite Order, California-Arizona Province.
- Holy Land, Greece, & Europe Pilgrimage, August 1985, Holy Innocents Church, Long Beach, CA.
- Holy Land & Rome Pilgrimage, May 1985, led by Rev. Fr. William Fenton, O.C.D., Pastor, St. Therese Church, Alhambra, CA.
- Oberammergau Pilgrimage, 35th Anniversary Passion Play, September 1984 led by Rev. Fr. Manuel Guico, and May 1984 led by Rev. Fr. John Higson, from various parishes in Northern and Southern California.
- The 41st Serra International Convention in Rome, July 1983, Serra Club Pasadena and other members, led by Monsignor Gary Bauler & Monsignor Paul Dotson.
- Holy Land and Rome Pilgrimage, May 1983, led by Rev. Fr. Manuel Guico, Holy Trinity Church, Los Angeles, CA.
- Holy Land & Europe Pilgrimage, October 1982, led by Rev. Fr. Ronald Seidl, C.Sc.R., St. Mary's Whittier, CA.

- Carmelite Pilgrimage - First International Congress of English Speaking Secular Members of the Ancient and Discalced Observances of Carmel, celebrating the Fourth Centenary of the Death of St. Teresa of Avila, September 1982. Participants from all over the United States, Ireland, and the Philippines, led by Carmelite priests and nuns.
- Holy Land & Europe Pilgrimage, August 1982, St. Stephen's Church, Monterey Park, CA.
- Holy Land & Europe Pilgrimage, October 1981, led by Rev. Fr. Corsinio Legaspi, St. Bruno's Church, Whittier, CA.

Below are some comments from *Littleways* pilgrims:

- "All you had to do was divide the tour cost by the number of days after you subtracted for the airfare. If a person would agree to do this they had to realize they were enjoying hotel, bus and food costs that an individual could never duplicate on his own." (A. & E. Bohorfoush, Bellevue, WA)
- "That pilgrimage was the best I've ever had. It was a spiritual feast for me. The food and hotels were also excellent. Thank you." (A. Mauney, Banning, CA)
- "It is unfortunate that we always have to come back to the real world, but what memories we have for the rest of our lives! You are so organized and efficient. Thanks for all your hard work. Because of you we were all blessed. Because of you we all have grown." (R. Barton, Sherwood, OR)
- "I just wanted to drop you a note to thank you for making the pilgrimage so unforgettable. I respect and admire you for organizing everything so well and for maintaining your sense of humor and sanity throughout. God has truly chosen the right person for this vocation. You will be in my prayers and I hope our paths will cross again in the future. God bless you." (T. Best, New York, NY)
- "I just want you to know that nobody could have done, organized the pilgrimage, better than you did. I thank God and St. Thérèse for all your efforts." (F. Torres, Chatsworth, CA)

- "As a tour guide, coordinator, nurse & friend, you are the best. No word can describe your strength, courage and patience that made our Pilgrimage of St. Thérèse the great success it was." (C. Goller, Glendora, CA)

- "I am still thrilled that I was a part of the wonderful Pilgrimage to Lourdes - planned by Bishop Joe and you. I don't know how it could have been more perfect." (M. Molander, Downey, CA)

- "Just a note to say very many thanks for your care, kindness and excellent leadership in a never to be forgotten pilgrimage." (J. & M. Gannon, Torrance, CA)

- "You were somewhere between our guardian angel and Mother Superior, with such grace and tact. This is not a job for you, Terri; it is a vocation and not a vacation!" (M. Gerich, Encino, CA)

- "My friend at work asked why I was so quiet. I said my body was here but my mind was still traveling through my memories. Thanks for the memories!" (T. Cardinali, Alhambra, CA)

- "How you could have done more for us would be difficult to imagine. I was the eldest member of the group (83 yrs. of age!), with constant watchfulness of my comfort and with every request granted me, what more can I say." (M.C., Salt Lake City, UT)

- "I want to say that both my wife and I enjoyed the tour through the Holy Land immensely and due mostly to your tremendous effort and organizational talent." (P.G., Tulsa, OK)

- "I want to thank you for allowing me to go on your pilgrimages. I believe God used you as the tool that allowed me to flourish spiritually, and as a result I am continuing to share all that I've learned with the many people God puts in my path." (L. Aceves, Los Angeles, CA)

- "A note to once again say 'Thank you' for the hundred and one plus things you did to make the trip to Lourdes so special. I'm offering a Mass for you that God will continue to give you strength to help many more pilgrims." (Bishop Joseph M. Sartoris, Archdiocese of Los Angeles)

Notes

Page 5

1. Jesuit Communications, 2013, *The Word Exposed* http://www.jescom.ph/?s=april+7%2C+2013

On February 11, 2016, on the Feast of Our Lady of Lourdes, I met Cardinal Tagle in person at the Manila Cathedral where he celebrated Mass for World Day of the Sick. I mentioned to him about this book, and he gave me his blessing and verbal permission to quote from his homilies. A photo of this precious moment when I met this holy man can be found in Littleways' Facebook page. https://www.facebook.com/Teresita.Terri.Ong

Page 8

2. Richard Morgan's "Remembering Your Story" was very helpful in creating my spiritual autobiography. Vinita Hampton Wright's "The Art of Spiritual Writing" also helped me to "craft prose." Information about these books are in the Bibliography.

Page 14

3. Rev. Fr. David Guffey, CSC, who is in residence at my parish, brought to my attention the importance of aunts and uncles in the family institution. He has been very encouraging to me from the initial stages of my writing this book. He is the National Director of Family Theatre Productions, based in Hollywood, California.

Page 34

4. This parish offers many opportunities to all ages and walks of life. Under the spiritual leadership of Monsignor Lloyd Torgerson for more than 3 decades, all are welcome in the community whose mission is "to form loving disciples who will transform the world." www.stmonica.net

Page 52

5. Pope Francis, 2014, *Francis - Daily Meditations – 2014* http://w2.vatican.va/content/francesco/en/cotidie/2014/documents/papa-francesco-cotidie_20141002_we-all-have-an-angel.html

Page 62

6. Rev. Ronald Rolheiser, OMI, "The Single Life" (*The Tidings*), 22. With permission to quote granted by Ronald Rolheiser. This article can also be viewed from his website – http://ronrolheiser.com/the-single-life/

Page 81

7. Society of The Little Flower, *St. Thérèse Frequently Asked Questions* http://www.littleflower.org/therese/st-therese-faqs/

Page 83

8. Susan Annette Muto, 1985, *Celebrating The Single Life*, 72 © 2002 Epiphany Association. With permission of the Epiphany Association, 820 Crane Avenue, Pittsburgh, PA 15216-3050. All rights reserved. For this usage only.

Page 84

9. It has not been determined who wrote this, but it has been credited to Mother Teresa of Calcutta, who was canonized by Pope Francis on September 4, 2016. The Holy Father said there may be difficulty calling her "Saint Teresa" due to her holiness being so near to us that we may continue to spontaneously call her "Mother."

10. Pope Francis, 2014, *Francis - Daily Meditations - 2014* http://w2.vatican.va/content/francesco/en/cotidie/2014/documents/papa-francesco-cotidie_20140123_hearts-free.html

Page 88

11. Pope Francis, 2015, *Francis - Letters - 2015* http://w2.vatican.va/content/francesco/en/letters/2015/documents/papa-francesco_20150328_lettera-500-teresa.html

12. Fr. Donald Kinney, O.C.D., 2015. *Carmelite Friars (Discalced) - California-Arizona Province of Saint Joseph* https://www.facebook.com/DiscalcedCarmelites

Bibliography

All information listed below are from actual edition used by the author of this book, even if there may be more recent editions by other publishers. Online resources are current as of the writing of this book, but can be changed by site's owners without notice.

Associated Press. 2014. "Jobless data help lift most stocks (Market Roundup)." *Los Angeles Times*, March 7: B4. Accessed March 7, 2014.

Bach, Richard, and Russell Munson. 1970. *Jonathan Livingston Seagull.* First Printing, January, 1973. New York, New York: Avon Books.

Frankl, Viktor E. 2006. *Man's Search For Meaning.* Boston: Beacon Press.

Jesuit Communications. 2013. *The Word Exposed.* Jesuit Communications Foundation, Inc. April 7. Accessed April 7, 2013. http://www.jescom.ph/?s=april+7%2C+2013.

Kinney, O.C.D., Fr. Donald. 2015. *Carmelite Friars (Discalced) - California-Arizona Province of Saint Joseph.* March 11. Accessed March 11, 2015. https://www.facebook.com/DiscalcedCarmelites/photos/a.10151 159838366906.437624.115370761905/10152631527211906/?ty pe=3&theater.

Morgan, Richard L. 2002. *Remembering Your Story.* Nashville, Tennessee: Upper Room Books.

Muto, Susan Annette. 1985. *Celebrating The Single Life.* Garden City, New York: Image Books.

Nouwen, Henri J.M. 1989. *In the Name of Jesus.* New York: The Crossroad Publishing Company.

Ong, Teresita A. 1975. "A Cross-Cultural Study of the Social Expectations by Men of Women in Two Branches of an International Bank in Manila and Tokyo (Master of Arts Thesis)." Institute of Asian Studies, Philippine Center for Advanced Studies, University of the Philippines, Diliman, Quezon City, May 1975.

Peale, Norman Vincent. 1952 and 1956. *The Power of Positive Thinking.* Greenwich, Connecticut: Fawcett Publications, Inc.

Pope Francis. 2014. *Francis - Daily Meditations - 2014.* Libreria Editrice Vaticana. October 2. Accessed October 2, 2014. http://w2.vatican.va/content/francesco/en/cotidie/2014/documen ts/papa-francesco-cotidie_20141002_we-all-have-an-angel.html.

—. 2014. *Francis - Daily Meditations - 2014.* Libreria Editrice Vaticana. January 23. Accessed January 23, 2014. http://w2.vatican.va/content/francesco/en/cotidie/2014/documen ts/papa-francesco-cotidie_20140123_hearts-free.html.

—. 2015. *Francis - Letters - 2015.* Libreria Editrice Vaticana. March 28. Accessed March 28, 2015. http://w2.vatican.va/content/francesco/en/letters/2015/document s/papa-francesco_20150328_lettera-500-teresa.html.

Powell, S.J., John. 1989. *Happiness Is An Inside Job.* Allen, Texas: Tabor Publishing.

Rolheiser, OMI, Rev. Ronald. 2013. *RONROLHEISER, OMI.* October 27. http://ronrolheiser.com/the-single-life/.

—. 2013. "The Single Life." *The Tidings,* November 1: 22. Accessed November 1, 2013.

Saint-Exupéry, Antoine de. 1945. *The Little Prince.* Translated by Katherine Woods. Harmondsworth, Middlesex: Penguin Books Ltd.

Society of The Little Flower. 2016. *St. Thérèse Frequently Asked Questions.* http://www.littleflower.org/therese/st-therese-faqs/.

St. Teresa of Avila. 1985. *The Collected Works of St. Teresa of Avila.* Translated by Kieran Kavanaugh, O.C.D. and Otilio Rodriguez, O.C.D. Vol. Three. Washington, D.C.: ICS Publications.

St. Thérèse of Lisieux. 1996. *Story of a Soul.* Translated by John Clarke, O.C.D. Washington, D.C.: ICS Publications.

Wikipedia. n.d. "Great Recession." Accessed 2015. https://en.wikipedia.org/wiki/Great_Recession.

Wright, Vinita Hampton. 2013. *The Art of Spiritual Writing.* Chicago, Illinois: Loyola Press.

Appendix

The Vocation to the Single Life
By: Susan Muto, Ph.D.

Jesus was single - a truth we hardly hear in church. The single life can indeed be a genuine path or vocation, a special spiritual calling, a way of holiness. In this article I will speak to the concerns and needs of single persons in the Church today and how they can be a special blessing in our families and parishes: in their single-state they represent and embody receptivity and availability.

In a society that tends to be couple-oriented, there are many who see their singleness as only a transitional state rather than as a potential life-time vocational call. Until recently the Church itself, in its prayers, programs, rituals, symbols, readings, and social gatherings, seemed to concur with the feeling voiced by many that being single was more a transition to marriage than a vocation in its own right.

In the research I did to write my book, Celebrating the Single Life: A Spirituality for Single Persons in Today's World, I learned already in the 1990's that persons who are single by choice or by circumstance feel at times marginalized, alienated, misunderstood, forgotten, or tolerated and without the equality in dignity everyone deserves. In questionnaires I gave to a group of fifty singles from ages eighteen to sixty, the following concerns came to the fore:

CONCERNS PERTAINING TO ISOLATION AND LACK OF DIRECTION

Society lauds the value of bonding and family affiliation. Why do singles have to be thought of as loners on the outskirts of familial commitment? Why do we treat singleness as a state of life to lament rather than a way of being to celebrate, as a cause for self-pity rather than an expression of other-centered, inclusive love?

CONCERNS REGARDING MINIMAL SUPPORT

Many of the singles I interviewed admitted that they would like the Church to become more proactive toward them by, for example, balancing its "marital mentality" with a complementary blessing of their vocation to the single life. They wanted to be motivated and inspired to deeper faithfulness to Jesus Christ as the model for single living in the world. Most concerns centered on their needs for understanding and spiritual guidance. How could they, as single Christians, maintain their commitment to Gospel values in a world inundated by careerism, consumerism, materialism, hedonism, and secular humanism?

CONCERNS FOR COMMUNITY AFFILIATION

A faith community is important to everyone. Longing for affiliation with a community is an oft-repeated concern. Many reported moving from church to church and even seeking non-denominational associations to find a supportive faith community. Divorced and separated persons and those with sexual orientations that preclude traditional "marriage" often feel alienated from the institutional Church. Due to the mobility factor built into many career tracks, single persons often lose their communal connections to the extended family and lament not finding in their church a true "faith family."

SINGLENESS: LIFE-GIVING AND INCLUSIVE LOVE

Singleness is an option for wholeness, a gift women and men bring to the Church, a capacity for respectful relationships modeled on Christ's own capacity for friendship, a call to inclusive love.

The root of the word "religion" means "to bind together again." Relation is the opposite of isolation. The Church is called by Christ to address every person's need to belong, to be befriended. Such a vision illumines the redemptive role of the Church as a herald of God's saving love for people of every age and situation. The Church is the family of God, many who happen to be married. One lifestyle is not of less or more worth than the other. Every human being is uniquely loved by God and created in His image and likeness.

Our faith tells us that we are formed by God and for God. Before one is a priest or a parent, a career woman or a nun, a person married with children or widowed—one is a single human being, uniquely created by God and called by name. In this regard, I would venture to say that single persons witness to the mystery of transforming love singularly taking place in every person's heart and in the world at large. The point is, we are born single and we die single. No one, not even the best of lovers, can die our death for us. Before we choose any other state of life, we are single. We are to celebrate the blessings of our uniqueness within the common bond of our membership in the human community and the body of Christ, his Church.

MINISTRY WITH SINGLES

The hope of singles I interviewed is that members of the Church dialogue with them to find new ways to be supportive of this vocation with its limits and blessings. In sermons and catechesis, pastors and the people of God ought to address issues of transitional, circumstantial and permanent singleness. Study groups can take up the task of analyzing the demographics of a congregation to see who is in need of this ministry. How many people in the pew are living in traditional family situations or not? Who is reaching out to single people who live together out of wedlock? What about our single elderly? Do we show them the love and care they need? Do we talk and pray about the way to remain a fully sexual man or woman and yet not indulge in sex for pleasure only? How do we help singles to integrate their sexuality and their spirituality and to see that chaste loving is a way of life, not an unreachable ideal? There are myriad ways in which our faith community can offer more support for single persons. Allow me to suggest some practical and effective starting points:

In Prayers of the Faithful be sure to include references to single as well as to married life.

Establish support groups for those who are single by choice or by virtue of transition.

Empower single adults through spiritual conferences, directed retreats, and sound preaching to develop a doctrinally sound approach to sexuality.

Stress the model of Jesus, his capacity for warm friendships with women and men.

Address directly through public forums and private consultations the sexual, social, and spiritual issues associated with separation from one's family of origin, and give special attention to persons in failed relationships, to one-parent families, and to those bearing children out of wedlock.

WHAT SINGLES CAN DO

Single people know that no human institution in and by itself can resolve the problems of loneliness, rootlessness, and an unhealthy questioning of their lifestyle, to say nothing of the problems associated with uncommitted relationships. That is why it is not enough to ask what the Church can do for singles. We must ask what singles can do both for themselves and for the Church. A good place to begin is to articulate the spirituality of singleness and its practical applications in Church and society.

Before recommending any model of restoration and redemption, it is essential for singles to renew appreciation for their own vocation and to promote an understanding of it. This goal can be reached in three ways:

REFUSE TO CONCEDE TO HAVING AN INFERIOR STATUS IN CHURCH OR SOCIETY

Single persons must try to do whatever they can to overcome prejudices directed at them and to reaffirm their worth and dignity as persons. Similarly, no person should be denied a position or function in society because he or she is single. Issues of justice apply to all, including equality in pay and working hours.

SEEK WAYS TO OVERCOME INJUSTICES LINKED TO NOT BEING MARRIED

This might mean taking a stance against economic structures that show preference to persons who are married rather than single. It may also mean not marginalizing "them" into "singles groups" or efforts to "minister-to-singles" as persons who are "other than" or "different from" the rest of the "church family."

PROMOTE A SENSE OF INCLUSIVENESS AND AN APPRECIATION FOR ONE'S GIFTS

Warm, vivacious, fully alive, and single people need and want to be included in worship services, committee meetings, parish councils and social gatherings. Singles can become proactive in this regards by offering, for example, to do substitute parenting or grand parenting, to visit the sick and to use their gifts for friendship by reaching out to other marginalized people in the community.

A SPIRITUALITY OF SINGLE LIFE

Thus far we have seen that it is a misconception to identify the single vocation mainly in reference to marriage—as if to be single has no identity of its own. This line of reasoning inevitably relegates singleness to a second-class position. Because singleness predates marriage or community membership, it must not be defined depreciatively as a state of "not being" but appreciatively as a state of "being" to be celebrated in its own right.

I can vouch from my own experience that it is unwise to allow oneself to drift half-heartedly into the single life without reflecting upon and praying about what it means to find oneself single in the world. Do I see this vocation as a meaningless burden, devoid of life-giving potential, or as an invitation to commit myself to a faith-filled life open to God and others in joyful self-giving? Lacking this kind of reflection, being single can open one to the traps of self-centered preoccupation or sensual indulgence. Hence, even when personal options are limited by circumstances beyond one's control, one has to choose either to celebrate being single in joyful surrender to God or to grow bitter because of it.

The spirituality of the single life enables one to be more present to others. In married life this outreach of love is admittedly restricted by the primary responsibility to one's spouse, children, and immediate family. As a single, one experiences a certain latitude in responding to the call to love and serve whomever God sends.

There are several ways in which single persons can celebrate their spirituality, advance their faith, and enjoy the fruits of commitment to Christ.

Love Chastely, Love Generously. To live with Christ is to witness to the wholeness of being a male or female person who manifests self-respect and respect for others. The love singles show if they are growing in intimacy with God ought to be non-possessive, non-manipulative, self-giving, and compassionate. Charity means trying to love others with the love with which God has loved us. Hence single persons in the Church have to set and maintain high standards to exemplify the art of loving.

Be a Friend. Friendship in the single life calls for relaxed detachment from exclusivity for the sake of fostering affectionate, inclusive loving and firm commitment to Christ. The detached yet committed loving characteristic of spiritual friendship is only attainable to the degree that we open ourselves heart and soul to the all-inclusive love of Jesus. Friendship of this sort leads to a quality of encounter that fosters uniqueness of personhood while opening us to the communal side of life which opens us more fully to God and others. This faith enables us to talk to "soul-mates" about our hopes and fears, our successes and failures. Together we can pray that God will guide the decisions we make and the actions that follow from them. We trust that God will befriend us as we have befriended one another.

Be Open-Ended. The single life has open-endedness about it that may plunge one at times into ambiguity and puzzlement. We may find ourselves asking in our twenties and again in our forties: "Am I really called to stay single all of my life or is my being single merely due to a set of circumstances over which I had not control?"

Live in Attached Detachment and Detached Attachment. These two dispositions help single people not to give in to the myth of omni-availability, as if they have no life of their own, especially where family members are concerned. One must be willing to convey firmly yet gently to relatives and friends a need for privacy and solitude that ought to be accepted.

Be attached and detached at the same time. After all, mothers and fathers, brothers and sisters, coworkers and church members for the most part act out of good will. There is simply a fine line between caring for us and trying to control us.

Recognize One's Vulnerability and the Need for Forgiveness. All human beings are vulnerable, but the state of feeling broken and in need of healing may be heightened in single life. We need only to think of the pain occasioned by a divorce that began with a severe betrayal of fidelity. Nowhere is this vulnerability more obvious than in the sexual realm where single persons out of loneliness often expose themselves too soon to intimate contacts that may yield pleasure but do not offer lasting joy. We must be as gentle towards ourselves when we err as God is gentle towards us. For how is it possible to show compassion for the faults and mistakes of others if we have reserved none of it for ourselves?

The heart of the single person must become more and more one that listens to the needs of others while admitting one's own woundedness.

Compassion of this kind is patient and peaceful, it fosters the gift of spiritual generativity, whether one is a biological parent or not. To touch without crushing, to temper anxiety, to hold tight and know when to let go, to forgive as we have been forgiven—these are the hallmarks of the single vocation Christ calls us to live in the light of his own dying and rising.

CELEBRATING SINGLE LIFE

Living in singleness strengthens our desire to be more receptive to God's will for us. It increases our courage to stand up for what we believe and not to be caught in churning tides of popular opinion. Christian values will always pose painful questions to a society that mocks commitment. Choosing to live as a single person faithful to the call of Christ means exposing oneself to the possibility of hurt and pain, but also to the grace of hope and peace.

Recall the lives of single Christians like Søren Kierkegaard, Dag Hammarskjöld, and Flannery O'Connor. Their singleness made them especially available to witness to Christ in philosophical, political, and literary realms. They suffered misunderstanding, but they were not afraid to stand up for what was right and to defend their faith. Such freedom carries with it a high degree of responsibility. One must be ready to proclaim one's beliefs, to take a few extra moments to listen to people and to respect the dignity of everyone. How else can one become a healing presence in a broken world? We can allow God to use us as instruments to bring about this transformation, for in our singleness we are free to flow with God's will in the situation where God places us; we are free to travel lightly and go where God most needs us to be.

As Jesus walked along the road to Emmaus with two seekers, so we must walk with Him by walking with others. By sharing our burdens and sorrows, our blessings and joys and letting them share their own experiences, we companion each other on the way. Together we realize we are all single and unique yet at that same moment never alone. He is with us always!

"I will let fall from heaven . . . a shower of roses."
St. Thérèse, The Little Flower

Littleways

www.littleways.com
www.facebook.com/Teresita.Terri.Ong
E-mail: showerofroses@littleways.com

Made in the USA
San Bernardino, CA
05 October 2016